Raising Happy Kids
on a Reasonable Budget

Raising Happy Kids on a Reasonable Budget

PATRICIA GALLAGHER

Copyright © Patricia C. Gallagher

This Edition 2001 - Special Edition for Baby's First Book Club® Bristol, PA 19007

Raising Happy Kids on a Reasonable Budget. Copyright © 1993 by Patricia C. Gallagher. Printed and bound in the United States of America. All rights reserved. No part of this book may be reproduced in any form or by any electronic or mechanical means including information storage and retrieval systems without permission in writing from the publisher, except by a reviewer, who may quote brief passages in a review. Published by Betterway Books, an imprint of F&W Publications, Inc., 1507 Dana Avenue, Cincinnati, Ohio 45207. 1-800-289-0963. First edition.

   02 03 04 05   5 4 3

Library of Congress Cataloging in Publication Data

Gallagher, Patricia C.
    Raising happy kids on a reasonable budget / Patricia C. Gallagher. — 1st ed.
       p.   cm.
    Includes index.
    ISBN 1-58048-203-1
    1. Parents — Finance, Personal.   2. Home economics.   I. Title
HG179.G26   1993
640'.42 — dc20   92-40297
                                                        CIP

Edited by Donna Collingwood
Designed by Sandy Conopeotis

ABOUT THE AUTHOR

After leaving her corporate position at AT&T to care for her children at home, Patricia Gallagher decided to combine her business savvy with her love for children. She began a child care center out of her home and has turned the years of experience into six books, numerous journal articles, pamphlets and publications.

Trisha holds a BA in Early Childhood and Elementary Education and an MBA in Finance and Management and has enjoyed many professions, including elementary school teacher, college instructor, preschool director and day care mother.

Trisha has been a featured guest on the "Oprah Winfrey Show," "Sally Jessy Raphael," "Maury Povich," "People Are Talking," "Hour Magazine," Financial News Network and CNN. Articles about Trisha Gallagher's expertise have also been featured in over 100 national and local magazines and newspapers.

Trisha Gallagher and her husband, John, reside in Richboro, Pennsylvania, with their four children, Kristen, Katelyn, Robin and Ryan. She is the creator of the "Send a Team of Angels to Help Movement."

ACKNOWLEDGMENTS

So many people have shared their ideas with me during workshops, interviews and friendly conversations. I would especially like to thank Cathy Skwars, Kate Smith, Florence McLaughlin, Eunice Vandine, Patti O'Connell, Terri Griffin, Pam Soda, Mary Ellen Gerlach, Priscilla Huff, Diana Giannaula, Joann Hinkle, Susannah Thomer, Kathy Pagan, Jean Ludington, Doris Patterson, Claire, Sarah, Jan and Kathy Mohan, and Ginnie and Paula at the "Once More Shop" for sharing all of their great ideas. Donna Collingwood, my editor, has been wonderful. She has the natural ability to put herself in the role of a penny-pinching parent and posed all the right questions. I am grateful for her dedication to this book.

Introduction

This is one book I never expected to need (let alone write). Having a family alters a life-style, as my husband and I found out in 1982. Just a few short years ago, we were a two-income family with no kids. When the mothers of young children in my neighborhood talked about coupon savings, special sales at the department store on Little Tikes play equipment, or how they discovered an inexpensive way to make a holiday craft, I never realized how vital these timely tips were to their financial health. Now, as a stay-at-home mom with only a husband's paycheck to make ends meet, my eyes have been opened and I have mastered every trick of the "penny-pinching parent trade."

Trying to save a buck is not a new hobby I developed late in life; it is simply a survival technique employed while trying to feed, clothe and provide for a family of six. The reality of providing for necessities in the 1990s is that no manna falls from heaven, at least not in my hometown. Cutting, pasting and collecting ideas from friends and neighbors, newspapers and magazines became a pastime, one that proved both profitable and fun. Who could offer better advice as mentors than others who were actually making ends meet on a finite income?

The suggestions in this book are paramount to survival when living within a budget. Oh, how things change when you simultaneously add one baby to the family and go from two incomes to one! As proud first-time parents, we felt Robin was the most darling baby in the world and we have since added Katelyn, Kristen and Ryan to our family. No doubt we "struck gold" with a wonderful family but our bank accounts still reflect a decline in net worth.

There may still be a few people who are financially secure and have that nest egg put away for hard times—a wonderful position to be in. But even rainy-day savings can be wiped out with a job layoff, a health-related disability, a lawsuit or just a major home repair such as a new roof.

This book shares inside secrets to financial well-being. Apply these tried-and-true, practical tips. The savings may not buy a villa in Acapulco, but you may have extra money in your checking account at the end of the month. What a treat to send all of your bills out on time and have a few dollars left over to treat the family to pizza on a Friday night. For the uninitiated, this book will prepare you if times ever get tough and you search every pocket for school lunch money, look between every cushion for money to pay the papergirl, or scramble all over the station wagon looking for toll money.

The teacher in me wants to start off with a quiz to assess your strengths and weaknesses. How do you know if you need a crash course on money-saving ideas? See if you can relate to any of the following experiences shared by family and friends. Now several years after the fact, they are able to laugh about everything, but at the time they would have welcomed the useful information included in this book.

Have you ever . . .

- had the engine in your car go five days before Christmas?
- not been able to sign your kids up for sports teams because you didn't have the registration fee?
- paid for swimming lessons with your credit card?
- paid your child's school tuition seven weeks late after receiving several reminder notices from the school administrator (as if you really could forget!)?
- driven your car without insurance, not because you were negligent about sending in your premium, but because there just wasn't enough money in your account?
- not had any money to buy your daughter a birthday present?
- suffered with a toothache because you did not have dental coverage?
- closed your blinds and drapes when you saw the minister coming to collect for the annual charity drive?
- given someone a check and prayed all day that it wouldn't bounce?
- driven twenty-five miles to buy groceries to find a supermarket that took a credit card?
- paid for milk, apple juice and diapers at a convenience store on a Sunday night with pennies found in your top drawer (and prayed that your neighbor wouldn't be standing behind you waiting in line)?
- been declined use of your credit card in a discount store with a long line of angry shoppers behind you and a full cart in front of you?

This little test wasn't meant to depress you, but most people can relate to some items. At one time or another in your life, you will need to know that one way to make money is by saving money. The people who candidly shared those experiences are not from a poverty-stricken, third-world country but from middle-income, nice suburban areas located near Los Angeles, Princeton, Philadelphia and Washington, D.C. If some of these situations sounded all too familiar, you are not alone.

There are dozens of innovative ways to stretch your buying power. In the pages that follow, you will find advice from the experts — other parents like you who are living on a shoestring budget but doing their best to make it stretch. By thinking creatively and applying my own family-tested, penny-pinching princi-ples — bartering, swapping, grow/make/do-it-yourself and some simple fix-up techniques — you will be able to cut expenses and save on the cost of raising a family.

CHAPTER ONE

Feeding Your Kids

I have a confession to make. It's embarrassing to admit as the author of a book about pinching pennies that I at one point had second thoughts about the value of couponing.

True-blue coupon clippers will gasp as I relate this event, but the purpose of this confession is to let you know that in the beginning it may seem like "work" to get your couponing system in order. I can assure you, though, that it is definitely worth the extra effort. Within the first few weeks of clipping, sorting and filing in a coupon box, you will gain momentum and will feel victorious when you reap the rewards of great savings at the checkout counter. You will have won the all-American game that is played daily throughout the country: the grocery store that charges outrageous prices vs. the struggling family trying to make ends meet.

My venture into the couponing arena began just before I had my third baby. With thirty-five extra pounds of baby on my normally thin frame, I was feeling irritable and tired. With my semisorted, haphazardly arranged coupon system, I attempted the awesome task of shopping for a family's groceries on a Sunday afternoon, peak crowd time.

After an hour of comparison shopping and trying to think like a tightwad, I surrendered! I abandoned my two overflowing carts filled with groceries and left the store, close to tears. "This coupon shopping is for the birds. You would have to be out of your mind to do all of this to save $35 a week," I thought in exasperation. I went home and asked my husband to return to the store and finish the shopping mission. And although I'll tell only my closest friends and you, I didn't even give him the coupons, rebate slips and shopping circular.

Since at that point I had not mastered the couponing game, it was easier to ask him to retrieve the carts, write out a check and bag the goods, all purchased at full price. I'll excuse myself by saying it was merely an amateur's attempt to coupon. I wasn't truly organized in the beginning and the task was frustrating. Postpartum, with another hungry mouth to feed, I began couponing in earnest.

NEWFOUND MONEY — LITTLE WAYS TO STRETCH FOOD DOLLARS

There are two ways to add more money to your food budget. You can either earn more or you can save more. I recommend the latter. I have tried both ways and saving money in little ways adds up to big savings.

What are little ways? Well, as an example, I remember visiting a friend's house as a teenager. I was horrified to see what a "cheapskate" her mother was. Today I admire her thriftiness and have even adopted some of her cost-cutting measures. In addition to saving a few dollars, she was being environmentally aware by recycling twenty years ago. She reused plastic sandwich bags after simply rinsing them out and letting them air dry. When a family member couldn't finish his or her dinner, it was wrapped with plastic wrap, labeled with the person's name and into the freezer it went until a later date. (In our family, leftovers were usually tossed into the bowl for Aloysious, our family pet, or just thrown into the garbage, although I am sure they really could have been another meal.)

My mother-in-law had some depression-wise ideas that were filled with budget brilliance! She saved quart milk cartons, margarine and cake containers for her storage needs. Rubbermaid and Tupperware containers could offer nothing more than her cast-offs in terms of saving leftovers. She even planned her day to save gas as she ran errands. Empty containers doubled as vases, pots to start seeds and even as miniature terrariums for the grandchildren. Bruised fruits and wilted vegetables were not thrown away but creatively used to make some delicious dessert or casserole. She opened her paper napkins and ripped them in half. Two squares were used at a time instead of four squares — a simple way to get twice as much value for your money.

In Europe, people use cloth bags for every shopping trip. No need to destroy our limited forest resources just for the luxury of a fresh brown shopping bag for each foray into the supermarket. Paper bags and plastic bags can be used multiple times at home also. You'll end up buying less plastic wrap for personal use.

Instead of using paper plates and plastic utensils for lunches and snacks, plastic plates and cups and metal utensils can be used. Washing dishes after each meal saves the expense of running a dishwasher and using detergent, and it actually saves time.

When it comes to packing the kids' lunches, skip buying the brown paper bags and let them take their lunch in a lunchbox. If they prefer the bags, ask them to fold the bag in their pocket after lunch and you can reuse it again and again.

Use cloth towels and napkins instead of paper. It is not much extra work to throw them in with a load of wash.

Reuse aluminum foil when possible or take your aluminum products to a recycling center and collect a few extra dollars. Even newspapers and glass recycled can offer some additional income.

Here are a multitude of food preparation tricks and money- and time-savers for you to try:

■ Baby food is extremely high priced. Use your blender to grind up a portion of the family meal and serve it to the baby (when it is age-appropriate or when your doctor advises you to serve baby food). Also, why buy individual jars of fruits such as applesauce for a baby when you can buy the regular size? Puree canned peaches and pears in the blender. You pay for the packaging when you buy small baby food jars.

■ For lunchbox desserts, cut your costs by separating the prepackaged snacks. Each child gets one, not two.

■ Buy a large bag of chips or pretzels and package it yourself in individual plastic bags.

■ Make several packages of gelatin or pudding at dinnertime. Serve some for dessert after dinner. Make several smaller servings and refrigerate in small, plastic margarine containers with lids. These individual portions are great for lunchbox desserts.

■ Make your own cupcakes from a packaged cake mix. It's a great way to satisfy the school kids — they love to help make them (lick the bowl, that is) and you can make a dozen for pennies each. Muffins are very inexpensive to make and more nutritious than cupcakes.

■ In the supermarket, take time to look at slightly damaged goods (set aside in a special area). The prices are usually slashed because the packages have been opened or dented while on the shelves or during shipping. Don't buy dented cans of soup or food packages that indicate they may have been tampered with or "sampled" by other shoppers.

■ Add a little club soda to orange juice to make it "fizz" and stretch the quantity.

■ Add a little more water than directed to canned soups.

■ Busy parents can put together casseroles and skillet meals quickly and economically. Look at the packaged dinners in the frozen food section of your grocery for ideas to create your own.

■ When making a dinner, double the recipe and freeze the second meal for one of those evenings when you don't have the energy to cook. Stews, casseroles, soups and breads are easy to prepare in quantity for a later meal.

■ Make a quantity of steak sandwiches or meatballs and sauce. Freeze several containers of each in individual portion sizes in a freezer-to-microwave container. In a separate bag, freeze rolls. If you do not keep the meat and rolls separate, the sandwich will be soggy. Hungry teenagers and husbands can just pop them in the microwave instead of calling the local sub shop and ordering home delivery (save that delivery charge, too!). Check your supermarket freezer section and mimic the sandwich types they offer frozen by making them at home using your own ingredients, like sausage and cheese on a biscuit.

■ Call your local U.S. Department of Agriculture's Agricultural Extension Service or Cooperative Extension Service listed in your phone book. The home economist on staff has a great deal of information about freezing meats and prepared meals. Ask to be put on their mailing list for recipes, food storage ideas and gardening tips. In particular, ask for any pamphlets about freezing main dishes and what foods can be safely frozen and for what duration. This program is funded by your taxes.

■ Make your own TV dinners by saving leftovers in individual serving sizes of meatloaf, mashed potatoes and cornbread. Never waste leftovers, just label them for contents and date and serve again. For real ease of preparation, freeze in a dish that can go directly from the freezer to the microwave.

■ Buy frozen juices and add your own water. Why pay $2.19 for a 64-ounce bottle of apple juice made from concentrate when you can buy a frozen can of concentrate for $.99 and mix it yourself (3.4¢/oz. vs. 2.0¢/oz.). Plus a 12-ounce can of juice is easier to carry home from the store. Buy several cans on sale and enjoy your savings for weeks!

■ Don't throw away the broth from roasts after you cook them. Save it and use it later for a soup flavoring. It adds a delicious taste.

■ Save your leftover scraps from vegetables and use for a nice hearty stew or soup. Use bouillon or roast beef juice as the basic liquid. Then dice meat such as roast beef and add vegetables.

■ Fresh vegetable salads, soup and warm Italian bread can be a very satisfying and inexpensive meal. Try different salads such as cucumber, endive and radish, and three bean.

■ Don't waste the fat after cooking bacon. Put it in a container for later use as a dressing for spinach salad. Melt the fat, add lemon juice, a dash of salt, sugar and some mushrooms. You have your own low-cost house dressing.

■ As an alternative to store-bought prepared salad dressings, make your own oil and vinegar dressing by putting mostly salad oil in a container and adding a little vinegar and spices to suit your taste. Shake it well and you have your own dressing for literally pennies per bottle.

■ My sister-in-law swears by making her own bread. She bakes in quantity and finds that the ingredients of flour, water, yeast, nonfat dry milk, sugar, salt and vegetable oil are low cost and produce a high yield. In addition to baking for her family, Sarah makes homemade bread as gifts for a special teacher, bus driver or just for a friendly "home from the hospital" visit.

■ Substitute margarine for butter when baking. For cookies and cakes, I have never been able to taste the difference and margarine costs much less. (Be aware that some recipes call for butter only and will not be the same with a substitute.)

■ Make your own pizza dough from a mix or from scratch. Just add your own sauce and cheese or add vegetables and meat. Pizza Hut and Domino's won't be too happy about it, but you can make your own large pizza and add multiple toppings for a mere fraction of the cost.

■ If you make coffee or tea in the morning and don't finish it, just put it in a thermos or insulated jug and drink it throughout the day, at home or at work. No sense using more electricity to heat it up or to make a new batch. By using a thermos, you are getting your money's worth out of tea bags and coffee.

■ Buy fruits and vegetables at a farmer's market or produce stand. Buy what is in season, at the peak of the season. If there is a high demand for the produce, the price will be high. I have found at roadside stands that the more tomatoes (or corn or apples, etc.) the vendor has, the better your chance for a bargain. Don't be afraid to "dicker." Remember, the farmer wants to sell out so that he does not have to carry his wares home again. Your ten-dollar bill will carry a lot more weight here than in a grocery store. Bargain by saying that you want to buy a bushel of strawberries and a half bushel of peaches and then offer a reasonable payment for purchasing in quantity. Fresh vegetables purchased this way are less expensive than canned and don't have the preservatives of frozen foods. If you must buy at a grocery store, look for specials and buy fruit and vegetables when they are in season. (In some parts of the country, produce purchased at a farmer's market may not be less expensive, but a greater variety of farm-fresh fruits and vegetables are available.)

■ Buy your meats and dairy products at a farm. In my area, you can buy fresh milk in a clear plastic bag as opposed to a plastic carton. It sells for thirty cents less than the standard gallon. Since we use about a gallon a day, $2.10 a week is saved or close to $120 per year. We have all heard of instant dry milk, but did you know that there is a noninstant dry milk? Most people say it tastes better than the other powdered variety and it is easy to mix using your blender. To see for yourself, call a wholesale dairy product store listed in the Yellow Pages.

■ You can usually get meats custom-butchered and packaged (quick-frozen also) to your specifications at no additional cost at a farm store in rural areas. You might have to drive a few miles from home to get these bargains but it is a fun trip. Be sure to take the kids along for a farm visit. To find out about the availability of farms in the area, you can inquire at the 4-H office sponsored by the county extension office, listed under the Department of Agriculture in the phone book. In some areas, they offer a guide that lists the farms that sell milk, lambs, produce, etc. The 4-H clubs are in close contact with farmers for their many joint-sponsored activities. You could also call the Future Farmers of America organization affiliated with the agricultural program at local colleges. Vo-tech programs at schools in rural areas would also be a source of information.

■ Veal is expensive. Chicken is a better buy. Make chicken parmesan by replacing the veal in the recipe with chicken. All other ingredients in your favorite recipe remain the same. Your family will probably never notice the difference.

■ If you use a product a lot, such as soup or baked beans, buy large multiserving containers rather than several small cans. My family loves fruit cocktail so I buy a jumbo size and put it in small margarine containers, which the kids take to school for their dessert.

■ Make a quick and easy blender soup with leftover vegetables. Use a half cup of cooked vegetables to one cup of broth or consommé. Blend on low speed and heat before serving.

■ Don't cook too much of a first-run (never-been-tried-with-your-hard-to-please-eaters) dinner entree or other new recipe. Kids can be finicky eaters — you might have a freezer filled with tuna chowder in multiple containers that the kids decided they didn't like on the first night. By the following summer, you finally toss it. My advice is to cook adequate portions unless you are sure that it is a tried-and-true dish.

■ Stretch your casserole portions by adding additional vegetables, rice, pasta or potatoes and substitute meats that are on sale for specific meats when possible.

■ Use a Crock-Pot. Purchase a less-than-premium grade of chuck roast when on sale, add vegetables, cook all of the ingredients all day and the result is a delicious meal. You can use a lesser grade of meat because by cooking it all day, the result is very tender meat.

■ When whole chickens are on sale, always buy at least two. Roast the two for dinner and slice one for a meal. With the bones and remaining parts, make soup. When the price is right, buy in quantities of four or five, cook them, and just slice the meat for sandwiches, a quick dinner or as a change of menu for school lunchboxes. This type of meat certainly costs less than when you purchase it by the pound at the delicatessen.

■ When the price of chicken is low, it's time to get out your cookbooks and experiment with some chicken a la king, chicken noodle soup and chicken croquette recipes.

■ If your family doesn't care for the dark meat in a sandwich, you can fool them by putting it in a food processor and with a few whirs of the processor, change the appearance. Mold a chicken croquette with the blended meat. By breading and baking the croquette and pouring a crème sauce over it, the meat will be sufficiently disguised.

■ When turkey is on sale, buy it, cut it up, use the backbone and neck for soup, roast the breast, make breaded cutlets from the thighs and whip up a vegetable stew from the legs. You could try the same with pork; with the skin and bone concoct a soup, make cutlets, and roll the rest for roast. When beef or chuck roast is on sale, cut away the bone and make soup, cut some meat up for stew and make roasts from the rest.

■ Make several mini-meatloaves instead of full-serving sizes. They cook faster, you don't use as much electricity and you can just put them in plastic bags and freeze. For a quick meal or sandwich, just thaw and prepare. I make ten to twelve mini-meatloaves at a time rather than the full size. (When ground beef is on sale, I buy in quantity.) The kids somehow eat even more when they are served in the kid's meal mini-meatloaf size.

■ When pot roast or eye roast is priced right, stock up so your family can enjoy cooked roast beef sandwiches on a roll. Once again, at the deli the price of roast beef is high. Cooking the roast yourself and slicing it at home is a great way to enjoy roast beef sandwiches cheaply.

■ Collect recipes from friends and look in magazines and newspapers for ideas for dollar-saving "Meager Meals." Try a new twist on a pasta dish or do something different with an inexpensive cut of pork, stew meat or hot dogs. Meager Meals are those you can make in a hurry, yet are nutritious and economical. Creamed dried beef sandwiches; bacon, lettuce and tomato sandwiches; grilled cheese sandwiches; pancakes; spaghetti and meatballs; cheese and noodle casseroles; stews served over rice, noodles or mashed potatoes; fruit and cheese; chili con carne; sloppy joes; omelettes; hot dogs and baked beans; and lasagna are inexpensive main dishes. To round out the meal, serve with lettuce salad and muffins or warm rolls.

■ About once a week, hold a "leftover" smorgasbord. As a kid, I thought it was pretty neat because it was served like a buffet and I could select whatever I wanted. This is a great way of using the leftovers.

■ Borrow cookbooks from the library. Or, shake the dust off the cookbooks you probably have at home. With an eye for creating some new dishes, you will probably be surprised at the treasures you already have in your own kitchen library.

■ Use powdered dry milk mixed with the directed amount of water as a substitute when making cookies, puddings and cakes. My mother "tricked" us for most of our elementary school years by filling a gallon container with half store-bought milk and the other half "homemade milk." The secret is to serve it ice cold or you might be discovered.

■ Don't purchase an excessive quantity of something that has a short shelf life.

■ If a few friends share your penchant for penny-pinching, you may want to start a food co-op. In this way, you can buy in quantity and share the costs. Volunteers need to buy and distribute the food to the members on a rotating basis.

■ And while on the subject of food, how about dog food? Our vet recommends the dry dog food, which is substantially lower in cost than the moist canned dog chow.

BULK BUYING

Buying in bulk can be a great way to stretch your dollar. The things to purchase in large packages or economy bottles are items you currently need and those items you'll definitely use in the future.

I have made some budget blunders in the past by buying several boxes of pancake mix, ketchup or cooking oil just because I had coupons or the price was a special one. Since I don't especially like to cook or bake, these items sat on the shelf long after the expiration date, so the bargain really wasn't a bargain for me.

Sometimes the store brand is actually the same as the name brand. In many cases, one company manufactures both products with the same ingredients. Only the label is changed! They ship the same exact orange juice or soup out to different companies. You could be paying extra just for the fancy or extra packaging or for the company's expensive advertising campaign.

For items such as frozen vegetables, sugar, flour and vanilla, I compare the ingredients and the price. I buy the store brand if it is the better value. My kids are especially mortified when they observe the store brand soda in my shopping cart or at home on the shelf. I just explain to them that if it tastes just as good but is less expensive, then that is what I am going to buy. It'll leave more money for other things. Even cheaper are the refreshing drinks made from powdered products where you simply add water to make lemonade, Kool-Aid, iced tea or grape juice.

My experience is that generic is not always better. Napkins and paper towels purchased in a plain black-and-white wrapper with the no-frills look are not necessarily of the same quality. What one name-brand paper towel might absorb in a hurry might take the work of ten sheets of a no-frill brand. Make a test comparison. It'll save money in the long run.

EATING OUT

Check your local restaurants for advertised specials. Usually one night a week is set aside for a special offer. Our family regularly goes out to eat at family restaurants: one fast-food restaurant offers the $2.99 unlimited salad bar and free iced tea refills; another has a special titled "Kids Pay What They Weigh" and free drink refills; a popular pancake eatery has a "Kids Eat Free Night"; and a fourth has an all-inclusive Special Kids' Meal. Certain conditions may apply, so call first for times and days and any other restrictions.

About a half hour before you leave for the restaurant, give the kids some yogurt, cheese, an apple or just a little something so they aren't completely starving when you arrive. This also helps to alleviate the begging for dessert, which is how some restaurants make their money. The special deals bring families in but the extra desserts, drinks and money to play the video games add to the cost of the meal. The desserts are often overpriced but look absolutely delicious. You also want to avoid ordering the extras so that less of a tip is required. This is one way to avoid spending more than you have budgeted for a night out at a restaurant.

■ When the kids beg to go to a fast-food restaurant while you are doing errands and it is around dinnertime anyway, put a limit on what you can spend and tell the kids what it is. Without a specified limit, you could easily spend triple your desired amount.

■ Take your own snacks when shopping at the mall. That way, you can eat one of your snacks while sitting on the bench or at the food court and just spend a dollar or so for a drink as opposed to giving in to pretzels, popcorn and candy bars, which can quickly add up.

■ Make your own popcorn and stop at the variety store for candy when going to a movie.

■ To celebrate a special occasion, go out for lunch instead of dinner. The meals are usually priced lower at this time of day. The decor is the same, the celebration is the same, but your check will probably be half the dinner price. Many restaurants have an early-bird special if you eat in the late afternoon hours or about 5 P.M., before the "dinner crowd" comes.

■ Keep your eyes open for the two-for-one entree specials that are often advertised in the newspaper. Restaurants offer these specials so that you become familiar with the restaurant and thus become a full-paying customer in the future. Try not to go for the extras such as appetizers or drinks or your bill will increase substantially.

■ Always inquire about specials when you call for a reservation. Restaurants want your business and may tell you of an unadvertised special. I recently did this and found out about an Italian Delight special meal, only it required a coupon from a newspaper I didn't have. I simply asked if they could make an exception for a family of six that wanted to eat there. You guessed it! No problem.

■ Another way to eat hearty and save simultaneously is to go to a happy hour that serves appetizers and a variety of snacks and hot and cold hors d'oeuvres. For the price of one drink or soda and a tip, you can engage in fun conversation with your spouse and sample the goodies from the happy hour buffet.

COUPON SAVVY

As you shop, you have no doubt noticed some of the elaborate coupon-clipping systems that people employ. I have a friend who, along with her husband, gave up well-paid jobs to start a new business. The downside was no income for a couple of years while things got off the ground. So she plunged headfirst into the world of couponing and rebating. She could be dubbed the Product Rebate Princess in her couponing circles, and as she shared her tips with her neighbors shortly after Christmas, she proudly held up for display a gift from her husband. Did you know that Black and Decker manufactures a battery-operated coupon clipper? We oohed and aahed appropriately (and laughed about the little black gadget that certainly was handy).

So for the tricks of this trade (couponing and rebating), here are some suggestions.

■ Scan the weekly circulars that arrive in the mail. Look beyond the obvious food store coupons for others such as dry cleaning, carpet cleaning services, chimney sweeping, free photos with Santa at a camera shop, etc.

■ Scan daily and Sunday newspapers and compare sales. Clip all the coupons of items you anticipate needing and determine if each one is a current need or future need. Scanning the food and retail store sales flyers first will prime you to clip and set aside those coupons you can use on your next immediate shopping trip. Then you won't have to hunt for them later.

■ Look in magazines for manufacturers' coupons.

■ Take the coupons you need and pass the circular along to your mother. She may like the coffee and pain reliever coupons while you can save a bundle on the cereal and diaper coupons she does not use.

■ Get together for tea once a week and exchange coupons with friends, a church group or co-workers.

■ Shop the stores that are offering case-lot sales or buy one, get one free. Buy only if prices are reduced and if you really can use the item. Let's face it, if sardines were available at five cents a can, it would be no bargain for my brood.

■ File coupons alphabetically or by aisle if you always shop at the same store. As you write your shopping list out at home, note the items that you have coupons for by putting an asterisk next to the product on your list. When you get to the checkout booth, retrieve the appropriate coupon from your file and match it to the item in your cart.

■ Take all of your coupons with you in a box sorted by aisle, category, store or product. When I mentioned using a shoebox to a friend, she laughed. She uses a big plastic container, the kind used to store sweaters. Her file system, divided by manila folders, indexed by cereals, toothpaste, detergents and paper products, etc., would never function in a standard shoebox. For some coupon shoppers, coupon billfolds, recipe card boxes and checkbook pouches are too small. If you don't take all of your coupons with you, you could miss some great savings.

■ If you have extra coupons that you won't be able to use before the expiration date, be a supermarket Good Samaritan and leave them on the shelf for some other penny-pinching parent.

■ Look for product rebate coupons in magazines, newspapers or on the store rack.

■ Shop stores that advertise double or triple coupons — but read the rules first!

■ Be aware that in different parts of the country, different marketing techniques are used to win your grocery business. Some stores offer no-frills shopping, lower prices and no coupons. Others woo you with coupons and price leader items that are priced low to lure you into the store. Popsicles may only be ten cents on a special sale, but the store is counting on you to buy many other items once you are in the store.

■ Don't offer to bag! Keep your eye on the cash register. Recently the clerk made a mistake. Instead of subtracting $2.00, he added it. Another time, instead of taking 25 percent off the purchase price of $9.99, the clerk deducted twenty-five cents. This mistake cost me about $2.25. By being vigilant and watching what the cashiers ring up, you can get the savings that are promised. It is much easier to catch mistakes as they happen than to realize it after you get home.

■ Spend about an hour a week organizing your coupons so you aren't fumbling through your pocketbook and backtracking through the aisles for missed bargains.

■ Don't be embarrassed to use thirty or forty coupons per order. If anyone seems to be getting irritated, it is probably because they are jealous . . . they wish they could be saving $30 or $40 per shopping excursion.

■ Save POP's (Proofs of Purchase) for known or potential rebates. Make sure you know what product, size, etc., they are from. Many premiums offered by manufacturers make great little gifts or stocking stuffers.

■ If you care to donate nonperishable food items to local food pantries for the needy, you can do as a friend does. She'll buy items on special, using a coupon, and obtain the product for free or at very little cost. That's stretching your food dollar to feed more hungry mouths! (Of course, you can do this even if you are not donating the food.)

CUTTING CORNERS WITH WAREHOUSE BUYING

The current rage in bulk purchasing and appliance buying is the rapidly growing phenomena of membership clubs, factory outlets and warehouses. Familiar names in membership warehouses or wholesale clubs may be Makro, Pace, BJ's Wholesale Club and Price Saver's Wholesale Warehouse Club. There are many others that usually require a membership fee, but once you are a card-carrying member, you can purchase at prices substantially below retail. They offer a wide variety for business and personal use. In most cases, they keep their costs low by offering self-service and a pleasant but not fancy shopping environment. The goods offered are usually shipped direct from the factory without a middleman as in department store shopping.

A friend bought an exercise machine at our local warehouse for $50 less than at a regular store. Detergents, cereals, tires, gardening supplies, small and large appliances, electronic equipment and bags of food for your freezer are competitively priced. Also consider buying the store brand of many items such as detergent, paper goods and drug store items. You can pay your membership fee as an individual but check with your employer, credit union or business organization. My husband's benefit department will waive membership fees for employees of his company if they want to shop at the local branch of a national warehouse. A relative belongs to a senior citizen group that offers membership. Almost any group "qualifies" for membership. Just approach the store manager and ask for a group membership for any organization that you belong to.

A cookie outlet in our area sells bags of broken cookies and other snacks. My kids don't complain about that and the price is right. Pepperidge Farm outlet stores are great places to buy snacks for lunch boxes or a cake for unexpected company. A large bakery makes huge commercial-size cheesecakes and chocolate yule cakes. Their primary customers are restaurants but if the cake has a crack or some other minor flaw, they can't sell it. Perfect for my family, though, and for just a few dollars we have a cheesecake that could serve twenty guests. We don't mind the crack because we can just slice it into small pieces. Add a cherry topping to a cheesecake with a crack and no one will ever know! Check around in your area. You can look in the Yellow Pages of the phone book.

Many people have found that warehouse buying in the traditional sense (not the fee-based membership type plan) is a way to get more value for your dollar. A neighbor of mine goes once a month to a warehouse that sells frozen meats and vegetables. Although it is a no-frills facility and you must keep your coat on because it is like walking into a large freezer, where else can you get chicken for nine cents a pound and bags of frozen vegetables and cans of juice for a fraction of regular costs?

The way to find out about such places is to ask around. Feature articles in the food column of the newspaper, the phone book, junk-mail ads, the county extension office and shopper newspapers that most people throw away are excellent sources for ferreting out warehouse information. It is amazing what your friends and relatives do to save money, and just by exchanging ideas you can multiply your savings. But you don't need to shop warehouse style to use your freezer. Just buy a few extra bags of frozen veggies, cans of juice or pounds of meat (on sale, of course) and you'll have your own warehouse to "shop" from. Buying a large freezer when on sale or perhaps purchasing a used one from the want ads in the classified section of the newspaper is a way to save money and time.

FRESH AIR, EXERCISE AND FEEDING YOURSELF: HOME GARDENING

You don't have to have a green thumb or ten acres of land to supply your family with fresh, nutritious and delicious vegetables and fruits. A friend who is an experienced gardener enjoys sharing her enthusiasm for putting really fresh food on the table and in the freezer and jelly jars with everyone from Cub Scouts to retired folk. Here are some of her tried-and-true suggestions.

■ Gardening is for everyone, whether you live in the city, in a townhouse or suburban home or out in the country. Apartment dwellers with only sunlit windowsills, tabletops with plant growlights on them, or perhaps a balcony, can do container gardening and grow dwarf or basket-type tomatoes, cucumbers, lettuce and other salad vegetables, herbs and some flowers, to name a few possibilities. If you have a yard with a sunny spot, the possibilities are almost endless. Remember to start slowly with a few vegetables or flowers the first year and add new ones to those you like best.

■ Try planting vegetables like beans and radishes in succession, so you'll have a fresh supply for most of the summer. Planting a little extra will let you freeze or can some for winter use. Having just a batch or two to prepare is easier and appears less overwhelming than a bushel full from the farmers market (unless you have lots of willing help).

■ Fruits freeze and can well, and if you like jams and jellies, try making your own combinations. The new fruit pectins for jelly- and jam-making are easy to use and come in low-sugar versions, too. And, if your first attempts at jelly-making result in a soft-set, you can still use it as a delicious ice cream or pancake topping — no one will be able to tell it was supposed to be jelly!

■ When buying a quantity of fruit, look for local growers with pick-your-own operations. You'll get fresh, unblemished fruit in the quantity you want at a lower price. If they are located close enough, you can go there several times during the picking season for each fruit. Sign up for their mailing list so you'll know when the fruit is ready for picking.

■ Get the kids involved in gardening right from the beginning. They'll marvel at how carrots grow *in* the ground, and that fresh-picked peas eaten right from the pod as you pick are as sweet as candy. Sunflowers with heads as big around as a full moon that grow "sky-high" to a child will delight them and the birds. (If you want to eat the sunflower seeds, cover the head when the seeds begin to mature.)

■ A side benefit to gardening is the exercise and time spent with nature. After all my years of gardening, I still marvel at how a tiny "dry" seed can produce so abundantly. And that packet of seeds usually costs only a dollar or two. In my area, the grocery and garden centers both run half-price sales on brand-name seeds in February or March. So when those seed catalogs arrive in January, I make out my garden plan and wait for the sales. Write to seed companies such as Ortho, Burpee and Scott Lawn Products for free catalogs and planting guides. Your local gardening supply company can give you the addresses of their headquarters.

■ For the ambitious, you can start your own tomato, pepper, eggplant and cabbage plants from seed and save even more. Timing is important here because the plants must be just the right size at transplanting time; check a planting guide for approximate planting dates. An enjoyable project for the kids is to grow sunflowers from seeds. Those big plants come from little seeds purchased in the grocery store or a local garden supply.

When starting a vegetable garden, the easiest way to begin is with crops such as tomatoes, beans and peppers that are easily started by buying plants at a gardening center, farmers market or gardening store. Don't start these crops from seed for your first venture into gardening.

Cucumbers are easy summertime plants and can be started from seed on the patio. Radishes must be planted early in the spring, also from seed, and they tolerate cool weather well. Stringbeans, zucchini and squash are easy to start from seed, but care must be taken as to the precise planting time. Broccoli and cabbage are not for the first-time gardener.

The county agricultural extension service can advise you as to the optimum planting time for all crops, suggestions for pest-resistant crops (you don't want the ones that attract beetles), container gardening, how to concoct homemade, chemical-free pesticides, and the proper procedures to produce a lush garden. Their advice is free for the asking and they will provide a variety of booklets that tell you step by step how to plant a garden when you do not have much space, time, money or energy.

Consider growing herbs. Fresh herbs such as basil, dill, parsley and thyme will add a zesty taste to your cooking and a pleasant scent to your garden. Their needs are meager—just a little water and fertilizer. You can buy a tiny herb greenhouse kit at most garden centers. Alfalfa, soybeans and lentils can be sprouted inside and used as snacks, salad additions, or tasty ingredients for stir-fry dishes.

As you research and learn about the basics of gardening, it is necessary to prepare the land in advance for a good yield. Composting conditions the soil for planting. Building a compost pile consists of mixing yard scraps and kitchen scraps. And as unappetizing as this sounds, worms help in the aeration process of composting. Leaves and garden trimmings known as "browns" and kitchen scraps such as vegetables and coffee grounds known as "greens" all decompose quickly and are combined to make a soil conditioner that helps your crops grow. Do not use meats as scrap material in your garden because they will attract animals. Of course, do not put any diseased items in the compost pile because you will be putting unsafe material into the soil that will grow into your food supply. Dry, crushed eggshells are good material for your garden fertilizing process. Eggshells, vegetable matter and lawn trimmings break down naturally in your garden. With moisture and the contents of your compost pile, you have what it takes to get your garden off to a good start.

Libraries are an excellent source of information on gardening. Read several books about gardening and study the accompanying illustrations. It is easier to visualize the finished project with photographs or line drawings. There are even audio- and videotapes on gardening topics.

If you add up the costs of buying shovels, trowels, seeds and the extra water from your garden hose to water your garden, you may not be saving a bundle. Why not start a co-op garden with some friends and share all of the associated costs? In some towns, there are county-sponsored areas set aside for community gardening. The extension service can identify these areas in your locale. Write to Gardens for All, 180 Flynn Avenue, Burlington, VT 05401, for a free booklet that tells how to begin a community gardening project.

Some helpful books are:

The Complete Book of Herbs, Leslie Bremness, Viking. This book includes eighty recipes, expert advice on planting, growing and harvesting herbs, and ideas for aromatic decorations.

Martha Stewart's Gardening, Martha Stewart, Clarkson-Potter Publishing, includes one hundred seasonal recipes and lots of photographs.

Rodale Press offers a free booklet, *The Basic Book of Organic Gardening*, which explains chemical-free vegetable gardening. Send a postcard request to: Rodale Press, Circulation Department, 33 E. Minor Street, Emmaus, PA 18098. Mention this book when making your request.

There is no doubt in my mind, after practicing the advice I offer in this chapter, that you will see it is worth the extra effort to stretch your food dollar. If you follow the suggestions in this chapter you will have extra money in your savings account, too.

CHAPTER TWO

Clothing Your Kids

The eleventh commandment, according to Patricia Gallagher, should be, "Thou shalt never pay full price for anything." Why should you when you have end-of-season sales, rummage sales, designer warehouses, consignment shops, as well as several other alternatives? All you need is a little time and some advice from an expert on buying clothes for less.

Buying and selling at consignment shops is the key for the well-dressed, budget-conscious family. But for those who do not have access to or prefer not to shop this way, sewing your own and catalog shopping can offer great savings, too.

SECONDHAND STORES AND CONSIGNMENT SHOPS

The other night, I saw that a local church was having an end-of-season sale at their thrift shop. Whatever you could pack into a brown grocery-size paper bag could be purchased for three dollars. And how I love a challenge! At first I thought everything looked like it had been rummaged through, but upon careful inspection, I found lots of bargains. And, I did not buy anything that was stained, torn or looked like it had been used or abused!

You may not see anything that strikes your fancy at first, but before you depart, glance around one more time. If there is a large skirt that is made of attractive material, perhaps you can take it apart and make something for the kids or an apron for someone. At the very least, there could be all of the components of a good gypsy costume or a black leotard that can serve as the starting point for a cat costume. Or how about making a decorative pillow by cutting out the desired shape, inserting pillow foam, sewing up the sides and adding a little lace or trim? And finally, you can make pillowcases quickly from pre-owned sheets in good condition.

Be on the lookout for bargains wherever you go. For example, early this winter I passed a consignment shop associated with the University of Pennsylvania. A beautiful, black wool coat that beckoned me from the window now has a new home in my closet and I wear my $30 finery with pride.

Frequent consignment shops with the goal of becoming familiar with those that sell clothes in good condition (not torn, spotted or stained) so you don't waste your time rummaging through poor-quality merchandise. Occasionally, you will find a place that will allow you to return but that is not typical. (It's nice to be a frequent shopper so that when you ask for these special concessions, they know that you can be trusted.) Even within a small geographic area, quality and price can vary significantly. When the price is lower, the service is friendly and the merchandise is in good condition, you walk away feeling that you really got good value for your money.

You can't beat the prices you'll find at consignment shops for specialty items such as First Communion dresses, Scout uniforms, and dress-up costumes for a would-be ballerina or for Halloween. Instead of pulling together a plastic Mickey Mouse costume from the variety store, try to think ahead. Throughout the year, I buy used costumes in secondhand stores that were lovingly made by a talented parent. I have a costume drawer that holds a variety of great outfits such as a felt dinosaur, a fifties outfit complete with a poodle skirt, and a variety of furry, feathered creatures that can easily transform my kids into the recipients of Most Creative Costume Awards. The day following Halloween, most costumes and dress-up paraphernalia are discounted by fifty percent at retail stores.

When bargain shopping, if a garment doesn't fit, don't automatically put it back on the rack. Ask yourself if it is worth buying at the bargain price and then having it altered. I bought a beautiful Rothchild coat for my daughter. It was too short for her but had a large hem. I had it altered and it was used by three daughters consecutively. I recommend buying "quality clothing," especially if you plan to have more than one child. "Sunday-best clothing" gets infrequent wear and will undoubtedly be in mint condition for child number two.

Here are some tips for buying bargain clothing.

■ When clothes shopping for the family, try to find some items that can be worn "all weather." For example, I have a jacket that I can wear with a winter wool skirt or as a light cover-up with a summer dress.

■ Sometimes a beautiful outfit may have a stain (also look for missing buttons and broken zippers). Before purchasing, be sure that a professional dry cleaner can remove it or that you can at least camouflage it with a scarf or decorative pin.

■ Avoid outfits that require dry cleaning, especially for kids. Read labels carefully. Wash-and-wear outfits are desirable for kids — after one wearing, their outfits need to be laundered. Also, rather than wash a whole outfit, try to remove just the stain thus preserving the overall freshness of an outfit.

■ Buy items that fit you now. On a few occasions, I have made the mistake of buying slacks that were a size too small because I planned to lose five pounds in order to wear them. I don't need to tell you that this kind of reasoning is flawed. The five pounds less never happened and several pairs of someone else's beautiful pants still hang in my closet. (I guess it is time to sell them back to a consignment shop.)

■ Don't forget to check secondhand shops and rummage sales for pre-owned maternity wear, accessories, sporting equipment, ice skates, roller skates, ski equipment and furniture. You can usually find great buys on this type of merchandise, still in excellent condition. You may want to check the product recall lists to be sure an item is safe before buying, especially if it's an older item.

■ Check your favorite shops frequently. New buys come in every day so shopping at thrift shops can become a hobby or a habit. I want to buy the best articles before someone else does.

■ Don't buy what you don't need, although at times I have to remind myself of this. A suede skirt may be gorgeous and it might be a good buy, but it would not be practical for my life-style. It's something I do not really need, despite the bargain it may be.

■ When you see a great price on something you don't personally need at a consignment shop (or in a retail store), buy the low-priced items and put everything in a box labeled *gifts for the future*. Stock up on kid's umbrellas, stickers, washable markers, kites, colored chalk or beach towels.

■ Volunteer at a bazaar or thrift shop. In addition to feeling good about helping a worthy cause, you often have the opportunity to purchase the bargain items as they are displayed.

■ Tell your friends about consignment shopping. They may tell others who will in turn bring hardly worn goods into the store which may give you more of a selection.

CLOTHING BUDGET BONUS — SELL YOUR UNNEEDED ITEMS

If you have clothing or toys that are still in excellent condition, offer them to a consignment shop for extra money. Look in the Yellow Pages and call first to find out the store's policy for accepting clothes or other items. It is usually by appointment and yields a 50/50 money split, between the store owner and the consignor (that's you). If the clothes do not sell within a specified period of time, you usually have to go in by a certain date and reclaim them or authorize the shop owner to donate them to a charity.

Even if you are not interested in recycling your clothes for profit, pass along your toys, clothes, musical instruments and household goods to those who are less fortunate.

Since charity begins at home, round-robin clothes from cousin to cousin or around the neighborhood. In these hard economic times, most parents would be grateful.

Don't forget about the possibility of buying and selling musical instruments in these consignment shops. Sometimes there is a bulletin board where you can post an index card saying *flute wanted* or *piano for sale*. If not, place a classified ad in the local newspaper before paying full price at a store.

Organize a clothing exchange through your church, synagogue, school or parent organization. Be sure to include the concept of swapping computer equipment, games, software and Nintendo-type cartridges. Kids' videos and audio-tapes that your own children no longer enjoy may be valuable to someone else. You may sell items to each other or simply exchange. Most parents are just glad to know that someone is able to use what they no longer need. Teachers at a local elementary school bring in unneeded household items and children's clothes in good condition. When a local family is in need, the school nurse sorts through the "clothes closet" and helps the family out.

Where do you find consignment or thrift shops? Store names such as Worth Another Look, Sort of New, Once More, Bring and Buy, The Price Is Light and Top Drawer Distinctive Consignments are typical of consignment or second-hand shops. Many organizations such as the American Cancer Society and the Association for the Blind have thrift shops. Call local hospitals and churches to inquire if they offer special sale days or operate a full-time shop.

Check the paper, especially the free shopper variety. Also, as you drive around town, keep your eyes open for small signs advertising a secondhand shop.

Ask your family and friends for their personal secrets and for the location of consignment shops. Keep your eyes peeled for bargain shops advertised on super-market and church bulletin boards. At a few noncredit evening schools in our area, a fun two-part course in Thrift Shopping is offered. In the first class, thrifty tips are given and the second session is a "class field trip" on a Saturday morning to actually visit five shops in the area. The instructor puts together a bargain-hunter guidebook that lists regional consignment shops and the pros and cons of each. If there is nothing like this in your area, why not prepare this information yourself and offer a one-night class? It is a big hit in our area and the teacher makes a nice profit by selling her guidebook to the students.

OUTLET FEVER

Another form of stretching a dollar is shopping at outlet stores. Let the shopper beware! Just because something is marked discount, you cannot assume it is a great price. For me, stores such as Marshalls and T.J. Maxx are reliable for bar-gains, especially at the end of the season when a second sign indicates an addi-tional 60 percent off the already marked-down price will be deducted at the regis-ter.

Outlet stores can be of two types, manufacturer-owned stores or mass mer-chandise stores. At a manufacturer-owned store, the manufacturer of a product might have extra stock, slightly flawed merchandise or leftovers from a previous season. Their own stores sell the goods at a discount price, sometimes as much as 60 percent below retail. The Vanity Fair Outlet Store in a nearby suburb offers 50 percent off the retail price. As you can imagine, business booms especially at Christmas gift-giving time.

Mass merchandise stores, such as Marshalls, T.J. Maxx and Filene's Basement, on the other hand, buy the leftovers from a variety of sources and pass along the savings to you in the form of a large store selling many brands of clothing and housewares.

Some tips about outlet stores gleaned from my experiences should help you sort out their mysteries and let you get the most from your shopping trips.

■ Check store policies. If merchandise is returned, will you receive a cash refund, store credit or are all sales final?

■ Only buy goods that are today's fashions and are in great condition. If you are looking for something to match an outfit you have at home, don't forget to bring color or fabric swatches or you may select something that does not match and would be inconvenient or impossible to return.

■ Wear comfortable clothing and shoes if you are going to an outlet center. Tired and uncomfortable shoppers may make hasty and disastrous buying decisions (quite incompatible with the penny-pinching parent philosophy!). No-frills outlets may be in old overheated factories or inadequately heated factories. Make an informed decision as to how you need to dress.

■ Make sure your proposed purchases are really a bona fide bargain. Don't assume because they say it is that it is.

■ Pack a little bag with a snack or two and a drink. Factory outlets rarely have places to eat and smart shopping is hard work. You'll need some energy to search through the racks and handle the crowds. Usually you end up staying longer than you anticipate.

■ You can even be beautiful for less when you buy cosmetics and beauty supplies at a beauty supply outlet. Call a store that sells to beauty salon owners and ask if they sell to individuals. You will find a complete line of beauty/health aids and cosmetics. There may be slightly damaged makeup (like a cracked lipstick case) but for a price like a dollar, it won't affect the wearability. Look in the Yellow Pages under Beauty Salons — Equipment and Supplies.

■ When traveling, beware of outlet stores in foreign airports. I bought what I thought were authentic, beautiful handmade Icelandic ski sweaters during a layover at the airport in Iceland, only to find that I could have bought them for a lower cost on sale at a department store near my home.

■ Look carefully at the merchandise and be sure you are comfortable with the condition if it is marked "as is," "second" or "irregular." Since many items are overstock or factory seconds, make sure that the imperfection is something you can live with. If the item is intended as a gift, could you face the embarrassment if your friend returns it to you because the shoulders of the sweater you gave her are lopsided? (Yes, it happened to me.)

■ If you see an item that has a tear, a missing button, or a frayed seam, don't hesitate to ask if the store manager can give you another discount. It doesn't hurt to ask and they might say "yes." Just be sure you can and will make the needed repair.

■ Try everything on first. Sometimes in discount stores, the size tags are incorrect. The size 8 Liz Claiborne slacks that always fit you perfectly may really be a mismarked size 14 in an outlet store.

END-OF-SEASON BUYING:
MY FAVORITE PENNY-PINCHING ART FORM

I do love consignment shopping and outlet bargains, but the biggest thrill for me is when I can get new, brand-name clothing at better than secondhand prices. For me that happens at the end of each season. For example, about March 1, the department stores have their spring and summer merchandise displayed. Amidst the cheery Easter decorations, there is usually a lone rack or two in each department that advertises: *Pay your last respects, this merchandise must go, take 60 percent off the already discounted price.* One February, I bought my son's complete wardrobe for the next winter, everything including socks, pajamas, play clothes, his Christmas outfit and snowsuit. At regular prices, the register totaled $304, but with all of the markdowns, my receipt was less than $100. Of course, I hope I guessed correctly on what his size will be next year, but having had three girls before him, I have a pretty good idea of our family's growth rates. (If something doesn't fit, it can be given as a gift to a younger cousin or friend.)

Also, usually in February and March, you will find seasonal specialty items such as Christmas socks, red and green fancy barrettes, velvet headbands and dressy little girl's pocketbooks on a clearance table. (The wrapping paper, bows and decorations you can buy for a dollar or so now would be quadruple that price when everyone is buying during the holiday frenzy before Christmas.) Whenever I see a post-season sale with savings of 60 percent, I buy in quantity because I know, that with a large family, all of these items will be used either for my own children, their cousins, or given as gifts for the neighborhood birthday parties. As any mother of school-age children knows, it is wise to have a private stash of ready-to-wrap gifts on hand for those last-minute shrieks, "But Mom, I told you I was invited to a party and it starts in a half hour."

There are also discount stores such as The House of Bargains that sell brand-name clothes at discounted prices. They buy overstock from J.C. Penney, Sears and Osh-Kosh. I am on their mailing list, so I get advance notice of their sales, which often includes a coupon for special savings.

Occasionally, I have my heart set on an outfit that I love in a major department store but the price is out of reach. Before giving in to my wish for instant gratification, I ask the salesperson if there is going to be a sale. Since employees are just people like you and me, they want you to get the most for your dollar in these financially tough times. On many occasions, they will clue me in that the desired item will be 25 percent off starting on a particular date.

SO, YOU LIKE TO SEW?

With the high prices of clothes, linens and curtains, many people are going back to the basics — sewing their own. Look for fabric sales at local stores, but if you live near a garment center or a fabric factory, materials are a better buy there. The variety is magnificent and the prices low.

For drapery and large-item projects, garment center shopping offers great selection and price. A friend began to sew when she was unable to find flannel crib sheets for her baby. She took one of her fitted crib sheets to the fabric store, showed the clerk what she wanted to do, bought a piece of flannel in the recommended size, sewed a hem and ran elastic through it. Within an hour, she had made several custom-fitted flannel sheets.

■ Make your kids' shorts. Buy knit material that stretches so you don't have to have the exact size. The waistbands are just elastic, too. Make dresses with a large hem so can stretch a few seasons out of them by letting the hem down. To change the look for a second daughter who does not want a "hand-me-down" look, buy lace or a colorful trim and alter the appearance of a dress. We remade a First Communion dress by adding a few blue cloth flowers and decorative trim. The dress was then used for multiple functions, such as a graduation, an anniversary and Sunday church services.

Patterns are now available in a master size to accommodate many sizes. There is even a pizza cutter-like tool (rotary cutter) that makes it easier for the novice to cut material. Check your library for pattern loans since many patterns in fabric stores are not necessarily cheap. Eight dollars for a pattern plus the cost of materials does not make sewing a bargain for all clothing.

■ There is a toll-free number for the American Home Sewing and Craft Association that offers many services. Call (800) U-SEW-NOW and they will send you a list of sewing classes in your area. Your county extension home economics group also offers classes.

SHOPPING BY MAIL — A LUXURY THAT IS AFFORDABLE

If you hate malls and grimace in pain at the thought of in-store shopping in any form, then catalog shopping is probably right for you. Those who shop this way regularly say it is convenient, reliable and affordable. Just think, no traffic jams, no waiting in line and no rummaging through the racks. It is convenient to sit at home, not distracted by kids pestering you for drinks at the mall or overwhelmed by the racks of clothes and overstocked shelves that are in "real stores." Many items in catalogs are unique and many are not available in stores. I saw a pair of walking shorts in the Penney's catalog in every color imaginable from basic navy and khaki to salmon and teal. The actual Penney's department store did not carry these shorts. Although you may have to pay a small fee for major catalogs, the charge is usually deducted or credited against merchandise when you make a purchase.

Catalog companies also offer sales periodically, especially when seasons change. Examine a few issues over the course of a year, and you'll discover their patterns so you can shop them even more effectively. Fall catalogs usually arrive in early summer for a jump on back-to-school shopping before the stores are mobbed and the merchandise is priced high. Also by midsummer, many stores have a very limited selection of summer merchandise. Catalogs rarely run out of stock so that short sets, bathing suits and summer vacation wear can still be purchased in your favorite styles and colors by calling in your catalog order. Summer catalogs arrive in December so that summer clothing and resort wear for a cruise can be bought in the winter.

Some additional pluses are:

■ Most catalog shopping services have 800 numbers so you can really spend time with the operator taking your order, gathering information and getting your questions answered, without costing you money for telephone usage.

■ You can comparison shop by checking the price of an item in several catalogs. Catalogs often give an extensive description of features as to size, weight, color, etc. If possible, go to a trusted retail store and check out the actual item's physical appearance: brand name, style number, type, color and price. Don't forget to add a shipping charge to the catalog price. (Some offer free shipping.)

■ You can try on several items in the comfort of your home. In this way, you can see if the article matches your other clothing. You can try out ready-made drapes. If you are not satisfied, simply return them and get credit.

■ Since the items are mailed to you, you save time and gas by not commuting to the store.

■ The old standbys such as J.C. Penney, Sears and Montgomery Ward have served customers with reasonable prices for many years. In the past, they only offered their own brand of appliances. However, in order to compete, most catalogs carry name brands as well. There are some specialty catalogs whose prices are exhorbitant.

■ Check the Better Business Bureau, which is listed in the White Pages, if you have any concerns or misgivings about ordering.

■ The main catalog companies send main selection catalogs, but every two or three weeks they send sale catalogs that discount prices of many items in the main catalog.

Some cons of catalog shopping are:

■ Not all catalogs offer inexpensive merchandise.

■ Merchandise might not meet your expectations. The colors, fabric and overall quality may not be what you expected, so you have the inconvenience of returning the merchandise.

■ Some items may be back-ordered or out of stock.

■ You won't know if an item fits until you get it.

Questions to ask before placing your order:

■ How long does it take for merchandise to be delivered?

■ What is your return policy on catalog items? Make sure your money can be refunded or your account can be credited. (This question applies to in-store shopping as well.) Don't keep anything you don't like. The store wants you as a satisfied customer and most will accommodate you even if the outfit you return looks like you already wore it to a wedding.

■ What are the shipping charges?

■ Do I have to return it in person or can I mail it back? If I mail it back, am I reimbursed for the return postage? (Some catalogs send you a return label so that if you are not satisfied, you simply place the product in the same package, affix the label, call UPS for pickup and back to the store it goes.)

■ Beware of anything that seems too good to be true or is free. There is probably a hidden cost.

■ Be cautious when purchasing from television home-shopping networks. Be sure that the enthusiasm of the host does not convince you to part with your hard-earned cash for items that you do not need and may also be misrepresented on televison. In many cases, you may get a bargain because there is no middleman. Of course the above questions should be considered when shopping via electronic networks. I recommend paying by credit card rather than cash or money order because credit card companies will investigate problems and they have power with retailers. To find out about television shopping, you can call the Home Shopping Club, (813) 572-8585, or the QVC Network, (215) 430-1000.

The following books are helpful resources for mail shoppers. Check your library or buy the books listed and share the cost with a penny-pinching friend.

The Underground Shopper, Susan Goldstein, McMeel and Parker, Kansas City-New York.

The Wholesale by Mail Catalog, St. Martin's Press, 175 Fifth Ave., New York, NY 10010.

Shop by Mail Worldwide, Ann Flato, Random House, New York, NY 10022.

Some helpful resources are:

Fabulous Finds, Writer's Digest Books, 1507 Dana Ave., Cincinnati, OH 45207.

The Joy of Outlet Shopping, P.O. Box 7867, St. Petersburg, FL 33734

Outlet Bound, P.O. Box 1255, Orange, CT 06477.

Ask them to send you a schedule of the times when particular merchandise is sold.

■ If a problem with any company or merchant arises, contact the Consumer Protection Agency in your state. They investigate shady operations.

CHAPTER THREE

Educating Your Kids

Parents have to decide on the type of formal education they want their children to have, be it public, private, religious or home schooling. With the advent of two parents in the workplace or single-parent households, day care centers and nursery schools are flourishing. Many parents are faced with critical decisions. Opting to pay tuition for parochial schools or to enroll in no-tuition public schools often becomes a financial decision. If you decide on the private school, your budget is tapped twice, once for the "for fee" education and the second for school/property taxes.

MONEY-SAVERS FOR THE EARLY YEARS

Did you know that you could negotiate tuition for private school? The following examples prove that if you want something, it doesn't hurt to ask—you just might get what you request! A friend offered to use his fund-raising expertise to help the school administrator and, in turn, he received a reduction in tuition. Another friend noted in a newspaper article that enrollment was down at his alma mater. He contacted the school president and struck a mutually beneficial arrangement. By showing copies of his past tax returns and the high expenses that he incurs raising five kids, he demonstrated that he couldn't afford the regular tuition for his daughter. The college reduced it to "special family rate" and increased enrollment by one.

Remember financial aid isn't always based on financial need. Nurture and encourage any special interests or talents you observe in your child. Colleges and high schools hold sports, music, theater and community activities in high regard when evaluating applications. A boy I know who lived near the New Jersey shore was a great surfer. His years of practice earned him a college scholarship for a school in Hawaii. Another friend has a son who is a great soccer player. His parents asked his grade school soccer coach if he knew of any special scholarships based on talent, not on the family's need. The coach pointed them in the direction of a private junior high and high school and also told them the questions to ask and the benefits of enrolling. He was awarded a scholarship to begin in seventh grade at a private boys' school.

In addition to formal education, there are other areas of skill development in a child's life. Unfortunately, lots of these fun, extracurricular activities are costly. In many school districts, the budgets are shrinking. As a consequence, many worthwhile activities must be cut to contain the tax rates. The threat of cuts for sports, hobby clubs and other extracurricular activities has put some of the burden on parents.

You can help with fund-raisers to support the kids' activities. Be active in your parent-teacher organization. Be attentive to school happenings in the newspaper so you are prepared to act when a critical budget cut is proposed. In one school district near my hometown after-school bus transportation, cheerleading, team uniforms and football now are funded by the parents of the children. It's up to the parents to "fill in" (with time and money) where restructuring the budget has "taken out." One mother could not afford the money required for her daughter to participate in a parade in a distant city. She offered to accompany the band and to chaperone the outing. Her daughter was able to go without paying the expenses for the bus and hotel.

Work experience and responsibility add to your children's education. Give your kids a head start on learning responsibility by encouraging paper routes, baby-sitting, car washing, government jobs for teens and fast-food restaurant employment during the school year as well as summer vacation periods and holiday breaks.

There are ways to allow your children to learn, either during or after school, without spending a lot. And some of these activities can even help them get into college.

The early years is the time to impress on children the importance of keeping their grades respectable. Saving their own money and budgeting allowances, with some put into savings, is also good practice for the future. Here are some innovative solutions and get-ready-now tips that might help you save money in one way or another right now . . . so you don't have to pay as much later.

Bartering + Creativity = Extracurricular Fun

When I was about eight years old, four mothers in my development exchanged services or "teaching" duties for their four daughters. My mother gave sewing lessons and another offered baking lessons once a week. I still remember making a bathing suit and a skating skirt on which I lovingly handstitched a big white poodle. My mother even helped each girl make her First Communion veil with lace, beads and white netting. The cost to buy a similar veil would have easily been ten times what we spent by doing it ourselves. The third mom taught us gardening (both indoor and out) and the fourth took us to the library once a week. No money was spent to pay the teachers, and we learned so much during the after-school hours during third grade.

Think of your talents and how you might exchange services on a regularly scheduled basis. It could be once a week or once a month. Try the "Parent Talent Swap" for a semester. Have an informal get-together with a few moms and plan your events. As an example, you might elect to do the "baking tour of duty" from

September until December. By sharing talents with neighborhood children, your youngsters will learn new things, the cost will be minimal (supplies), and you will be getting free child care. You only have to plan for a two-hour activity but you get six additional hours of free time when your neighbors are sharing their interests with your child. The following semester, from January until June, you could try four different activities.

Do you think you don't have any special skills to share or talents that would interest your neighbors? Sorry, I can't let you off the hook that easily. You don't have to be a world-class ballerina or ice skater to share the simple things of life with kids. So what could you do? An example of some activities could be:

■ Contact your high school aquatic office or school administration office and inquire about the availability of a recreational swim at the local high school. In our area, the public school offers family swimming at a reasonable cost. On Friday nights, my kids swim with a neighbor's family for two hours, and on another Friday night I take their two children and two of my own children. (Be sure you feel comfortable with the swimming skill level of the kids you are responsible for and that you're a good swimmer.)

■ Another way to barter time is for parents to alternate going to a regularly scheduled activity such as a library bookmobile or story hour.

■ Think about bartering lessons in computer, ballet, gymnastics, exercise, gardening, sewing or woodworking.

■ Take the kids to sit in the audience of a theater audition or a choral society rehearsal. Go to a guided nature walk, a marshmallow and hot dog roast, or an outdoor concert. I find activities such as these in the calendar of upcoming events in my town newspaper. A quick scan of the "Things To Do" column could easily fill your kitchen wall calendar with ideas to explore, create and discover.

■ You could be the parent that plays board games with kids. (This I would personally welcome because I have never been able to sit still long enough to play Old Maid, Parcheesi, Candy Land, Monopoly or Fish. Lucky for me and my children, my husband enjoys such games and I get off the hook!)

■ Teach touch typing or keyboarding on your typewriter or computer. Better yet, borrow computer games from the library and challenge the kids. There are educational games as well as fun games for all ages.

■ Make ceramic crafts, paint T-shirts or do counted cross-stitch.

■ Start a holiday craft-making club. Make family door wreaths for all occasions: Halloween, Valentine's Day, Easter. The materials can be inexpensive. Check with your craft store for an example of a holiday wreath that kids can make. You can put this together for a couple of dollars per seasonal wreath.

■ Develop collections of some sort such as stamps, baseball cards, dolls or music boxes, and share this hobby with the kids. The United States Postal Service offers stamp collecting kits centered on a wide range of themes for a reasonable price.

■ Introduce the children to the rewards of volunteering at a nursing home or visiting a handicapped person. You can arrange to go weekly, monthly or on special holidays; or simply help out at special functions such as picnics or birthday parties.

■ Ask a local museum if they need volunteer guides for museum highlights and behind-the-scenes tours. This, of course, is if age is appropriate and if the composition of the group is mature and well-behaved. Perhaps with three children, this is quite workable.

■ Borrow language tapes from the library and practice conversational Spanish. Celebrate by going to a restaurant for Spanish food. Call the restaurant manager in advance and say that your "Language Club" would like to go on a tour of the restaurant. How could they say no, and wouldn't they have to offer you a sample or two? Or, gather the ingredients and have a party at home.

■ Borrow movies from the library and watch them with the kids. Make a big batch of popcorn and mix it with raisins or nuts for a change of pace. (Check out or send for Diane Pfeifer's book, *For Popcorn Lovers Only* (Strawberry Patch Publications, Box 52404-P, Atlanta, GA 30355-0404, $11.95), for great popcorn recipes.

■ Start corresponding with a pen pal. When it is your turn, help the kids make a project to send to the new friend. Send cards to veterans or a neighborhood serviceman or woman.

■ Exercise or play sports. Teach the kids a new game or skill.

■ Visit an alternative library at a free or nearly free museum, community college or cultural center. A recent call to a Polish Culture Center in our area introduced me to a wealth of information about cooking, history and schooling in this faraway land. They even offered us some special pastries that are popular in their country.

■ Don't forget church activities. I couldn't afford private singing lessons for my girls, but under the excellent training of their church choir director, they are getting excellent voice lessons.

The above ideas are simple to do and offer the same benefits of the more costly activities sponsored by community recreation centers or noncredit sessions offered by many colleges. However, if you do want to sign your child up for one of these higher-cost activities and are financially in need, remember that many schools offer "scholarships." Everyone understands that most families go through financial hardships at one time or another and most social organizations would be happy to allow your child to participate if need is demonstrated. All you need to do is ask. My children are enrolled in a summer Bible School for two weeks. The fee is a bargain at only ten dollars per child. When the administrator noted that I was enrolling three children, she told me that if the cost was prohibitive, they would waive it.

Another friend with limited income had twin girls. All of her friends were sending their kids to nursery school but she could not afford the tuition for the three-morning program. The nursery school charged her for only one twin but both girls were enrolled and enjoyed the program. My friend helped out as a volunteer as much as possible in exchange.

Tuning in to a Tutor

To pay a reasonable amount for your children to learn the basics of music, ballet, swimming or gymnastics, inquire about preteens or college students in the neighborhood who have taken lessons in the past and could share their talents. Two or three dollars an hour for a twelve-year-old instructor or $8 an hour for an older teen or college student is sure better than the $20 per half hour charged by many professionals. Take swimming as an example: even if you are not much of a swimmer yourself, a responsible older teen could give lessons while you supervise from the side. Peer swimming lessons are a good idea, and after the initial stroke instruction, let the maxim "practice makes perfect" take over.

Can't afford a tutor for your second grader? Does your child need help with math flash cards and reading? When your child has fallen behind in basic skills, it can become a true strain for an already busy parent. Chauffeuring a child to a tutor, waiting while the instruction takes place and paying one more bill or fee to pay may overtax your patience and pocketbook. You are often too close to the situation, and teaching your own child can become emotionally draining. It can be very difficult to switch from the parent role to the teacher role, both for you and your child.

This is where the beauty of hiring an impartial, outside-of-the-family sixth grader comes in. Someone a few years older than your child can do drill and mental exercises and even make the practice sessions fun. For a few dollars a week, I hired a teen as a private tutor. As I did homework with one child, she made the math drill sheet fun for another. And just think of how good the older child feels to have an opportunity to make a difference in someone else's life.

When my children wanted to take piano lessons, I dreaded the thought of buying a piano, nagging them to practice and whiling the hours away in the piano teacher's living room during lessons. My penny-pinching parent's solution was to hire a teen to teach the basics on the piano in her home for $2 an hour per child. After about six months, I could tell that there was genuine interest and at that point, I purchased a piano and started their real lessons. So far, so good, one year later!

Tutors can also be "in-house," given the right circumstances and personalities. For example, my friend was going to sign her eighth-grade daughter up for a summer algebra class. The location of the class was not convenient, but she was willing to drive twenty minutes each way and pay $100 for the special instruction. Unfortunately, the class was filled. Her solution to this dilemma—she "contracted" with her son, a high school senior, to teach his sister algebra on a regularly scheduled basis during the summer. As a result, there was no inconvenient commute to a classroom, no wasted gas or time, the son earned spending money, and most important, the algebra lessons were learned.

Where else can you find low-cost tutors? If it is a lesson in computers that interests you, check with a computer teacher at school. Perhaps the teacher is a member of a computer club and can point you in the right direction, or is interested in a "free-lance" assignment. Don't overlook college students as tutors. They can provide one-on-one instruction at less cost than the commercial tutoring centers. Even a patient senior citizen might enjoy helping a child learn, not only for the money earned, but also as an enjoyable way to spend time. Where can you find an available senior? Put a notice on a bulletin board at church, a retirement village, supermarket, nursing home or near a pharmacy where a retired person might go for medicine.

MONEY-SAVERS FOR COLLEGE YEARS

Before you know it, higher education choices must be evaluated. Many facts will be considered when you make this decision, including your (and your spouse's) educational experiences, the location and reputation of schools and your accessibility to them, and the costs involved (tuition, books, transportation, uniforms, etc.) to name a few.

And remember, not everyone has to go to a four-year college. The public community colleges and vocational institutes or trade schools are appropriate alternatives. Some benefits of community colleges are your kids can live at home, work part-time, don't need their own car and pay less per credit hour than some of the four-year institutions. You can even take basic college courses at a community college at less cost and then transfer the credits and your child to the school of his or her choice for technical or advanced classes. Be sure to check this out thoroughly first.

Offsetting College Tuition

It is in your best interest to learn as much as possible about money given to offset the high costs of education. Programs can be merit-based, need-based and non-need based. I hope the following information will aid parents already feeling a sharp pinch when they even think about tuition costs.

Some sources of information about money for college are:

■ Sun Features, Inc., Box 369, Cardiff, CA 92007: a guide to loans, scholarships and grants, called the *College Emergency Kit* ($5.50).

■ Life Insurance Marketing and Research Associates Association, Attention: Order Department, Box 208, Hartford, CT 06141: request booklet on college costs.

■ *Peterson's College Money Handbook* (Annual), Princeton, NJ. *Arco College Financial Guide Annual*, Prentice Hall, NY. *College Cost Handbook*, (Annual), College Entrance Exam Board of New York City. *The Scholarship Book*, Daniel Cassidy, (707) 546-6781.

■ Call (800) 4-FED-AID: ask for a guide that explains the grants, loans, scholarships, etc.

■ U.S. Department of Education, CIC, Department 506X, Pueblo, CO 81009: request information explaining Pell Grants, College Work Study Money and other helpful financial college-related information.

Other options worth investigating for loans, grants, scholarships and other tuition-reducing plans include:

■ Ask your bank about the Guaranteed Student Loan Program. Banks are currently subsidized by the government to process the paperwork for student loans; however, Congress may change this because the money banks receive for administering the program could be filtered into additional funds for students.

■ Inquire about Pell Grants, which were created about twenty years ago. This is the government's largest higher education aid program. These monies are given to low- and moderate-income students. You do not have to be poor to qualify.

■ Call (800) 824-7044 and inquire about PLUS loans. This is part of the student loan program set up by the Department of Education. This program allows parents of a dependent student to borrow money for college at a lower rate than banks with extended payback periods. As of this writing, the rate was variable, fluctuating with treasury bills, with a maximum interest rate of 12 percent charged for borrowed money.

■ Ask the school of your choice if they have any funds to help with other costs such as books and room and board. Perhaps your child could work on campus, as a landscaper, in the library or in an office, to defer these costs. Evaluate the costs of living on campus or off campus. Encourage your child to buy used textbooks rather than purchase new in the college bookstore.

■ Inquire if there is a discount or protection against future tuition increases if you pay in advance for a four-year program. You may pay in a lump sum and save money in the long run. How about some sort of payment on a schedule as an installment loan? It may cost a little more but you won't have to come up with all of the cash at once.

■ Scholarships are available even for those who do not have a financial need. Many schools offer merit money for those who are not in need but have something valuable to offer to the school. Financial awards can be given for leadership, sports ability and academic achievement. Be sure that you understand the length of the scholarship, i.e., is it for one year or four years?

■ Ask about any scholarships offered by civic groups, professional societies, women's groups, Scout organizations, the National Honor Society, the American Legion, the Elks, veterans' groups or your place of employment. To be eligible, you may need to meet specific requirements regarding grades, class rank, test scores or course of study. Affiliation or relationship with the organization may or may not be a requirement for application. In our area, the Pennsylvania Federation of Women's Clubs has established two Arts Scholarships in the amount of $1,000 each to be awarded to two graduating high school seniors. For information about union-sponsored scholarships, contact AFL-CIO, 815 16th Street NW, Washington, DC 20006.

■ Attend college fairs where student college representatives provide firsthand information about attending particular schools. Financial aid officers are often in attendance to answer questions and provide up-to-date information about student financial aid resources, how to maximize eligibility, and how to complete the appropriate applications.

■ Inquire at the schools of your choice for any scholarships based on merit in your field of interest, whether it be nursing, business or engineering.

■ Establish a good rapport with the people who work in the financial aid office of the college that you are interested in attending.

■ Talk to your banker or money expert about tax-deferred bonds and other financial packages that allow you to save for college now and pay taxes at a much later time. Attend financial aid programs that you see advertised in the local paper. Many people advise starting to save for college upon the birth of your child.

■ Sometimes if a parent works at a college, the children and/or parents can attend for free or at a great discount. Friends of ours were maintenance workers at a very fine college and their children received degrees at no cost.

With all these strategies, be sure you understand the rules and commitment required. For example, be sure to ask questions about the monies given. If an organization awards a scholarship for dance and your child no longer wants to major in that subject, what happens to the scholarship commitment?

Also beware of some financial aid or scholarship search firms. There are many fine groups, to be sure. Unfortunately, as with any business, a few have charged two of my neighbors and didn't pull through with the information guaranteed. These companies promise to help you locate money for school. In many cases, you could research this information on your own at the library or through government pamphlets. Some are well established and enjoy an excellent reputation, but I have heard some people say that they were not satisfied with the results. Check the references of the search firm for satisfied customers.

One final thought on financing your child's education: Pray a lot for yourselves and other parents and families who are grappling with the costs associated with sending kids to college. It can't hurt!

PARENTS AS STUDENTS

When it is your turn to learn something new, where can you turn? Whether you desire an advanced degree or would like to complete your GED for a high school diploma, it is never too late to begin. "Late bloomers" can earn additional credits that will enable them to enter rewarding careers and earn a decent salary. You may even be able to get college credits for life experiences so you aren't starting out on a freshman level. Check with the admissions office or adult education program director. And if you are a veteran, you are probably entitled to free schooling.

If you want to earn a high school diploma, contact the community college in your area. Often instruction and materials are free. Besides the obvious four-year and community colleges, check your area vocational technical school for courses that are fairly priced and offer a wide variety of in-depth training. You can start a new career in subjects such as air conditioning and refrigeration, automotive mechanics, computers, cooking, electronics, floral design, graphic arts, machine shop, plumbing, masonry, nurse's aide or health coordinator. Contact the National Association of Trade and Technical Schools, 2021 K Street NW, Washington, DC 20036 and ask for a free directory of accredited schools and courses.

Your kids often qualify for financial aid, but how about you, the parents? Save all of the forms for grants, loans and applications that your children get. You may qualify for many of the same programs. Many schools are trying to attract nontraditional students. Inquire as to the availability of any special scholarships. Many schools also offer a reduced rate for students over age fifty-five.

For information on older students, contact AARP Fulfillment, 1909 K Street NW, Washington, DC 20049, and ask for publications D12388, D13973 and D171.

CHAPTER FOUR

Keeping Your Kids Healthy and Well Groomed

A family that has managed the miracle of well-groomed children has achieved more than just good looks — good grooming habits are in the best interest of the family budget, too. Good hygiene and health practices result in fewer doctor and dentist visits and reduced health care expenses. The best insurance policy for healthy kids is a routine that emphasizes fresh air, plenty of exercise and relaxation. In today's fast-paced life-style, this is much easier said than done. Kids tend to follow the examples set by their parents, so put on your jogging shoes, cut down on sweets and visit your physician for regular checkups. The kids just might follow your lead if they see that good health and grooming are priorities for you. Washing hands before eating is one example of a good habit that with some gentle reinforcement can become a dinner-table rule.

To assure that your family adopts a healthy life-style, become the commander, drill sergeant, fairy godmother or the nagging parent — whatever it takes. I also recommend trying motivational methods, such as star charts that praise children for health habits they maintain on their own. Keeping physically and mentally fit, recognizing the negative effects of stress on the body, and eating and drinking sensibly are investments more valuable than gold.

DENTAL CARE

Taking good care of your teeth by brushing regularly and visiting a dentist twice a year can prevent serious dental problems later on. Before your child has his or her first dental visit, let him or her sit on the chair in the dentist's office for a few minutes after a sibling has finished treatment. This advance preparation and "getting used to it" before a real examination can help relax the child for the first time.

When selecting a dentist, be a wise consumer. Ask neighbors who they use and recommend. You will be surprised to find a wide price range for basic services such as fillings and cleanings. It is in your family's interest to shop around for competence and service when selecting a dental care professional.

A few other ideas to maintain dental health:

■ Ask your dentist about fluoride tablets or anticavity rinses.

■ Encourage the habit of flossing.

■ Give kids their own individual cup to rinse. Succumb to their diverse preferences for flavors including mint and even bubble gum if it means they will use it more often. If they like the taste, it might not be such a battle for you.

■ Make supplies convenient — keep extras in all bathrooms.

■ Buy a variety of colors, styles, shapes and character-type toothbrushes. Somehow if the toothbrush has a Christmas bear handle, a cartoon character or their name painted on the end, they are more willing to brush several times a day.

■ Teach children the money-saving tip of rolling the toothpaste tube from the bottom to get your money's worth and even to cut the tube in half when you can no longer squeeze any out. You can easily get another three brushings.

■ If you cannot afford dental care, call an accredited dental school. Services are based on what you can afford to pay.

HEALTH CARE TODAY

Is there really such a thing as low-cost health care? Programs do exist that assist people who need medical care and cannot afford to pay for it. Your child's school nurse receives information from Family Social Services regularly and can direct you to programs for physical exams and inoculations. Many public schools perform these services on site during the school day. County clinics offer medical services at no charge or on a sliding scale fee for those who cannot afford private care. Call county shelters and county social services. The staff has access to many directories that list services, twenty-four-hour hotlines and referral systems in your town.

Emotional health is just as important and there are many psychological services available. If you need help with drug- or alcohol-related problems, you can receive telephone help anonymously, if you wish. Caseworkers from the state Department of Health, Education and Welfare or the Department of Public Welfare offer programs on parenting in most cities. Even some of the major health carriers offer subsidized plans for those who cannot afford to pay for standard plans.

On the whole, health care is expensive and most people have the burden of paying for a substantial portion of it on their own. It is no secret that we are facing a crisis in health care. According to the Bureau of Labor Statistics, U.S. Department of Labor, the cost of medical care is 66 percent higher today than in 1982. The average amount spent on health care per year is more than $2,500 per person. You may think health insurance protects you from paying that amount, but, ultimately you do pay close to that. The hidden costs are reflected and passed along to the general population through higher insurance premiums, government taxes to fund Medicaid programs and deductibles that you are required to pay for your own care.

Budgeting for medical care is a fine idea, but one that is easily thrown out of whack come a season of ear infections so common with winter weather. Our family doctor charges $40 cash per visit for those who do not have HMO cards. Who can afford to spend $40 for each visit, especially if you have more than one child? Immunizations and prescription costs are in addition to the cost of the visit. Each of my four children averages at least four prescriptions per year. Doctor-related expenses can easily amount to $200 per month during the cold-weather months when ear infections, colds and flus are epidemic.

And don't count on the spring and summer months as times you'll save on doctor visits either. Accidents, such as splinters embedded in a knee, a bicycle mishap or a finger slammed in a door seem to increase with the temperature, and off to the emergency room we go. A few other calamities worth mentioning involve skateboarding, baseball, hockey and general roughhousing. It's uncanny how they occur just when you think you have a little extra in your checkbook. After the initial panic and concern for your child's welfare comes the reality of the emergency room's bill. My daughter's recent broken arm and associated medical care were billed at an amount comparable to what a relative spent on a recent vacation for two at a resort hotel.

Before rushing to the emergency room, place a call to your doctor. If the accident is not a life-or-death situation, it can be treated for less money in a doctor's office. Emergency room care is the most expensive option, and the doctor on staff will not be familiar with your child.

Accidents do happen even when parents are watching carefully. A few suggestions to minimize and prevent injuries are:

■ All children should wear bicycle safety helmets. Some states even require them by law. Teach your children the rules of bicycle safety such as to ride with traffic (walk facing traffic).

■ Keep bikes in good condition (don't buy someone else's lemon at a garage sale!) so kids don't lose their balance and fall because of a loose chain or a semiflat tire. A few lessons in basic bicycle repair is probably a good idea, too. Just as with cars, it is important to maintain the bike to avoid later problems. Give children limits as to where and when they can ride. One mother attached a fluorescent-colored flag with a pole to the tail end of her child's bike so the biker was more noticeable to motorists.

■ Accidents happen when kids are roughhousing. Establish and reinforce the rules of the house. No other kids allowed in the house unless a parent is home. No running in the house. Allow "gentle roughhousing" only in a certain room that has furniture with rounded corners, is padded and has no flyable objects within reach. (A mother with five boys suggested this one. I personally can't imagine dedicating a room for this but my only son is two years old.) Or only in the basement. Better yet, only outside.

■ If they play sports, make sure that children have a physical exam and the attending physician feels they are in good health before the sport begins. Provide proper equipment for safety: knee pads, elbow pads, shin guards, helmets, etc.

■ If you allow kids to use skateboards, mopeds or all-terrain vehicles, give them the conditions under which they may use them. If you give these items as a gift, make the safety equipment part of the gift as well. Make sure they receive proper and thorough instruction for use.

■ If you know that kids are going to climb trees, teach them how to do it safely. Examine the trees in your backyard to be sure they are free of nails (from a previous tree fort), and there is no poison ivy or thorn bush waiting to harm them.

■ Instruct children not to eat any wild berries growing in the area or touch any nests, wasps, bees or birds.

■ If kids are old enough to be left alone, teach them how to use the microwave if they have to cook something. It makes me uncomfortable to think of them operating the stove or oven even with a baby-sitter present.

■ Have kids play using the buddy system, especially when swimming.

■ Warn against talking to strangers. Role-play dangerous situations.

■ Keep your swing sets in good condition. Check for rust, missing screws and pointed edges. Swing sets are for swinging and are not to be used as monkey bars. (After two accidents within a year, we had to enforce this one.)

■ Keep a first-aid kit well stocked with gauze, adhesive tape, bandages, witch hazel and a first-aid ointment for soothing scrapes and cuts.

■ Keep emergency numbers (police, fire, doctor, hospital, ambulance and poison control) posted next to each phone. Accidents and emergencies don't only happen in the kitchen.

■ Take a Red Cross first aid course. It will give you a sense of confidence if an injury or accident occurs with your own children or anyone else's on your property.

Health-Maintenance Organizations

A variety of copay health-maintenance organizations (HMOs) have arisen during the past decade or so that promise to give members a break on the costs associated with family health care. So how do they work? Are they worth it? Are they beneficial for all? There are innumerable sponsors of plans, all plans are not the same, and they are modified continually. Make decisions based on your own family's needs and make a careful study of the options and limitations.

With an HMO plan, analysts estimate anticipated costs for a family in a given year. Using that information, they establish a dollar figure or premium to cover the cost of care. This premium is usually paid through a payroll deduction. The HMO is betting that they have accurately calculated the amount and that your medical costs will not exceed it. Thus, they make a profit. If you visit the doctor more than they have estimated and use an excess of services, then the health-maintenance organization may experience a loss.

There are many pros and cons to this system. With our plan, we receive a list of primary physicians and pharmacies. We select one of each and fill out the appropriate forms. Cards are issued that allow us to have unlimited visits for services and prescriptions as benefits of the program. In addition to the amount deducted from my husband's paycheck, we copay. This means we pay $10 per doctor visit and $5 toward each prescription. (These costs have increased since the plan's inception. Fees were originally $2.50 for an office visit and $2 for prescriptions.) My husband's company deducts a substantial monthly chunk from his paycheck for HMO and dental benefits. It is convenient not to have to carry money in your pocket for medical bills. There is something psychologically satisfying in showing a plastic card and paying merely a few dollars for care. Plastic cards do not seem like spending "real money."

Although HMOs offer some great benefits, there is a downside to my health-maintenance organization. I feel the bane of our system is its policy for referrals. Referrals have the ring of a permission note for someone who is not capable of making their own decisions. Call me an independent spirit, but who needs them? In our plan, you must obtain a referral from your primary physician before you are permitted to see a specialist. You cannot decide on your own to see the doctor of your choice, unless of course you want to be responsible for the payment.

I'd like to share one of my personal experiences. First, let me state that I don't feel that my primary physician looks kindly upon patients who wish to seek the opinion of a specialist. A friend in the medical profession explained that the primary physician is allotted an agreed amount of money for each family enrolled in his practice. Whether that family visits once or ten times a month, the amount the doctor receives remains the same. For each referral he authorizes for a patient to see another doctor, money is deducted from that fixed amount. Because the primary physician must relinquish some of "his" money to the specialist on my behalf, it seems that sometimes the best interest of the patient may be sacrificed in favor of keeping that money. Thus, permitting a referral becomes a monetary consideration in addition to one of patient care.

My baby was having stomach problems. As veteran parents, my husband and I felt something was seriously wrong. We had three other children and a pretty good idea about what was normal. We followed our pediatrician's medical advice for nine months, but the problem was not resolved. We felt that the doctor's diagnosis was faulty. I expressed my concern, based on my mother's intuition, and requested a referral to seek the opinion of a gastrointestinal specialist. The reluctant doctor told me the specialist would advise the same over-the-counter remedies we were currently using. Finally at our wits' end with our baby's painful condition, we demanded a referral. The first visit with the specialist sent us in a totally different direction, and within days, the baby was 100 percent better. The lesson I learned was to speak up and not be intimidated by a doctor. I also began to question the benefits of HMOs; I felt my son's quality of care was compromised because of my insurance carrier's policy in handling referrals.

I did a cost-benefit analysis and determined that, with the combined costs of the payroll deductions, the copay amounts and the associated prescription costs for the current year, it would probably have been in our best interest to pay as we went along. This is known as a *fee for service* basis. With this arrangement, you select the doctor, hospital and clinic, and as long as you can pay for the services, you have complete freedom of choice in the care your family needs. There are no hard-and-fast rules. My neighbor recently withdrew from her HMO. Her children are school-age and do not require as many visits to the doctor. But she felt that her prepaid service health plan was very beneficial when her children were young and prone to ear aches, colds, croup and colic.

In order to make the best choice based on your family's needs, be sure to ask questions before choosing a health insurance plan:

- How much will each visit cost? Is there a limit to the number of visits?
- Is there a copay amount?
- If a specialist is needed, will it be paid by the insurance plan?
- Are medications paid for? How many times can I refill them? Copay each time or just the first prescription?
- What hospitals may I use? Any limitations?
- What about emergency hospital care costs?
- Are any health care services for home nursing available?
- Are orthopedic shoes, eyeglasses, syringes, blood-glucose meters and the like covered?
- Are health classes, weight reduction seminars, exercise clinics or special services reimbursable?
- Are there are any discounts for nonsmokers and people who are involved in fitness programs?

General Health-Care Tips

Other insurance plans such as Blue Cross/Blue Shield and Medicare work differently, unless of course a particular plan adopts its own method of fixed-dollar cost or premium-based plan. Under the usual Blue Cross/Blue Shield or Medicare, you pay for visits to your doctor. The insurance pays the bill or reimburses you for a percentage of covered services.

Whatever your health-care situation, the following common-sense ideas will help you crunch the costs of medical care.

■ Question whether lab visits and additional testing, sometimes known as "defensive testing" in medical circles, are really necessary. (Excuse me for being a skeptic, but are the extra tests required for a diagnosis, to protect the doctor against malpractice or is someone trying to pad your bill?) A quote from an executive commenting on why the cost of health care is rising at an astronomical rate states one reason rather clearly. "Physicians are saying, 'If ten tests are good, twenty tests are even better because then you can defend yourself in court if the patient should decide to sue.' "

■ If a doctor recommends you see a specialist for an ailment, don't be afraid to ask if it's necessary. The doctor may then give you an alternative approach. This suggestion does not apply to any serious illnesses or complications. This penny-pinching parent dialogue is for concerns of a minor nature. Don't take chances or cut corners on serious medical problems!

■ If you are responsible for paying your own hospital bill, consider shortening your stay. Since you will be responsible for paying all the costs associated with your daily care, you want to leave the hospital as soon as the doctor says you are physically able. Perhaps you can come home a day or two earlier and save money by resting at home instead of allowing exhorbitant hospital-stay charges to accrue. There are many home health services that could supervise your care or perhaps a friend or relative could help out. Tylenol with codeine can be a high-ticket item at the hospital. Who needs to pay $4 for a pill you can take at home for much less? If a home stay is not possible, consider foregoing a private or semiprivate hospital room and request a ward that may have six beds in a room.

■ According to the Bristol-Myers Squibb Company newsletter, "Ninety-eight percent of hospital bills were found to contain errors; the average overcharge was $1,254." Check your bill and ask about anything that confuses you or seems like an excessive charge.

■ Contact the Visiting Nurses Association that is listed in the Yellow Pages.

■ Contact the public relations departments of health-care organizations and hospitals and request pamphlets on topics of interest to you.

■ Contact the YWCA and inquire about well-baby clinics and the services associated with keeping your child healthy.

■ Ask the school nurse to tell you of any programs that would help to keep your family in good health.

■ Speak frankly to medical professionals about financial problems. See if a solution can be reached based on a fee reduction or allowing payment over a period of time.

If You Don't Have Any Health Coverage

If you cannot afford private health-care costs or HMO plans, there are other avenues you can pursue to obtain health care for your family.

■ If at some point in time you need medical care and do not have cash to pay for a doctor's visit, explain your situation to the doctor. Ask the physician if he will provide care and then set up special payment arrangements to meet your needs. Many doctors have signs posted that state payment is due at the time services are rendered, but exceptions can be and often are made.

■ Contact your church when you need assistance with physical or emotional care. Thousands of local churches treat both the body and soul in these tough economic times. Many churches can provide referrals to appropriate clinics or direct you to financial assistance in issues regarding mental health, nutrition, substance abuse, prenatal care, vision and hearing screening, support groups and advocacy in health causes.

■ Medicaid programs are available for people with incomes at or below the poverty level. In most states, you apply at the local department of human services or social services whose telephone numbers are listed in the government section of your phone book. (This is not the Social Security office.)

■ Investigate county-run or government-subsidized clinics.

■ Call the WIC office, which stands for Women, Infants and Children. Women's health centers (associated with many hospitals), elementary school nurses, maternity care ward personnel, prenatal clinics, family doctors, county social services and pediatricians can give you the phone number of your local WIC program, which is government funded, as well as other helpful information.

Children who come to school hungry aren't usually healthy in mind or spirit. Studies indicate that children who do not eat breakfast before school can be inattentive, lethargic or exhibit behavior problems. A nutritionally poor diet leads to sickness and increases absenteeism. Nearly all schools are entitled to offer federally subsidized lunch and breakfast programs. Many eligible schools go without the subsidized programs because they did not request their share of available federal money.

Contact the U.S. Department of Agriculture or the Food Research and Action Group, an antihunger lobbying group. You do not have to be poor to qualify. As of 1992, any child from a family earning up to 30 percent above the poverty line qualifies for a free breakfast or lunch; children whose families earn up to 85 percent above the poverty line qualify for a reduced-price lunch. This program and many others that offer benefits associated with good nutrition can be especially helpful for low-income families, single parents and working parents.

If you find yourself in a food emergency, contact a service organization such as the Lion's Club, which, in our area, has a food emergency program. Families in need are not necessarily poverty-stricken. An unfortunate circumstance or situation such as a job loss or an employer delaying paychecks can leave you without food in your cupboard.

Prescription Pointers

■ Ask the doctor whether samples of the prescribed remedy are available. The sample may be enough to alleviate the situation, and you can see if it's effective before purchasing a quantity. Remember, the worst thing that someone can say is "no," and they just might say "yes."

■ Shop around for pharmacy prescription prices by calling four pharmacies listed in your area and comparing. You will be surprised at the range. I have found that discount drugstores are very reasonable.

■ Here's a shocker! According to a doctor I spoke to, there is a company that makes both the generic and brand name of a certain drug. Always see if there's a generic counterpart — it could mean a substantial savings.

■ Be sure to question the doctor if medicine should be taken on a full stomach, empty stomach, with juice, milk or water. When I was a teenager, I took tetracycline for years. I took the pills faithfully with a glass of milk at the prescribed time. Twenty-five years later, when one of my children was taking tetracycline, the doctor told me that milk products will cause this drug to be ineffective.

■ Also be clear about the shelf life of the medication. It could also lose its effectiveness under improper conditions — exposure to sunlight or storage at room temperature.

■ To save money at the drugstore, ask the pharmacist about comparative costs. If you are covered by a prescription plan, inquire as to the cost of the medication if you paid the full price versus the cost that you would pay with your prescription plan. The fluoride tablets I purchased on the plan cost me $5, which is the set fee for any prescription. The maximum quantity of vitamins permitted to be issued was fifty at a time (stipulated by the plan). The per-unit cost was ten cents per tablet. But, if I had purchased the same tablets without my plan, a bottle of one hundred would have cost $5. The cost for purchasing them without my plan's benefits was five cents each. How did I know to do this? The pharmacist suggested this comparison to me.

■ Check the store-brand aspirin price versus the name brand. If you look at the ingredients, you will see the formulas are identical in most cases and you can buy the cheaper of the two. Use this advice when buying sleeping aids, cold medicine, rash treatments, toothpaste, ointments, etc.

■ My doctor suggested an over-the-counter medication for one of my children. I had purchased this product for my older daughter several years earlier and I knew it cost a whopping $39. Since the maximum amount I would pay under my prescription plan was $5, I asked if there was a prescription remedy since I would prefer to purchase it through my plan. Fortunately, there was an equivalent so my out-of-pocket expense was $5 versus $39.

Home Remedies

In the not-so-distant past, people suffered from the same ailments as today but without all the popular over-the-counter remedies. So, what did they do? Herbs, lemon, chicken soup, healing plants, specially brewed teas and honey soothed the pain of colds, itching, infections and rashes. You can doctor yourself with these home remedies, or you can purchase the store-bought variety of pain-killers and infection fighters. The homemade remedies should only be considered for minor annoyances and discomforts — not for serious or life-threatening symptoms. You can find information at health food stores and herb shops. There are also books that offer recipes for relief of cramps, indigestion, motion sickness and other health problems. Of course, the penny-pinching parent considers both options carefully before paying for store-bought remedies.

Here are some of my favorites:

■ Canker sores can be soothed by placing a black tea bag, which contains tannin, directly to the sore.

■ Aloe plants are also considered by many to be effective in healing burns. Simply open a leafy portion broken off the plant and rub the inside moist area on the burn.

■ Headache? Try applying a cold pack to your forehead before you reach for the extra-strength pain reliever. Relax. Take a nap.

■ Can't fall asleep? Before you rush out to buy a sleeping aid, try a soothing cup of herbal tea. Celestial Seasonings teas are the brand that works best for me. Pleasant dreams and drowsiness also come very quickly after a cup of warm milk, hot lemonade, a warm bath or listening to soothing music. Avoid drinks with caffeine such as hot cocoa, tea, coffee and cola.

Prevention Techniques

Preventing an illness is the best way to save money as well as time and the aggravation of a trip to the physician. There are no guarantees of good health but studies show a sensible lifestyle and prudent habits help maintain it. Visiting a doctor regularly makes good medical sense because it enables a problem to be detected before reaching an advanced stage. Pediatricians often recommend that parents bring their children for "well doctor visits," which include a checkup or physical examination.

Unfortunately, when a child catches something, it is often times passed to a sibling or parent. Since no one fills in for parenting duties when the flu bug strikes, it is no picnic to play the difficult, dual role of "sick mom" and the mom who can do everything. Try to keep the sick person isolated from the rest of the group so that the illness can be contained.

Stress is known to weaken the immune system and exercise is one of the best stress-relievers. Work out before you decide that you need to medicate your anxiety. Don't pay for an over-the-counter tension reliever until you try this free remedy when the blues creep up on you. Get in the habit of biking, walking, jogging or working out. Fresh air and exercise improve mental health as well as muscle tone. There are several exercise programs on television. If the one you prefer is on at 5 A.M., tape it and do it when it's convenient. Or, borrow exercise videos from the library.

If you need the motivation of other people, join the YMCA or YWCA. You can exercise with others for a modest cost. (My HMO plan pays for this as part of my health package.) Most communities have low- or no-cost facilities available to residents. Or, save the fees and encourage a friend to join you in a game of tennis, badminton or just a daily brisk walk. Include the kids, too, in exercise programs, if you are sure that you can make the activities fun and not competitive. Adopt a "no-pressure environment" where "winning isn't everything" is the philosophy. Sports programs, scout activities, indoor winter swimming lessons, badminton, miniature golf, bowling and outdoor activities such as picnics in the park and running games (tag, tug-of-war and relay races) are enjoyable for all.

More cost-saving prevention tips:

■ Drink plenty of water to keep the body in good health. Fruit and vegetable juices are good choices also.

■ Keep inoculations up to date, such as those that offer protection from measles and rubella. Serious and life-threatening diseases can be prevented. Be clear about the appropriate timing for shots and oral vaccines.

■ A common-sense approach for maintaining healthy kids is dressing them appropriately for the weather. Protective rain gear is in order for inclement weather while hats, gloves and scarves (no matter how kids protest that they don't need them while waiting at the bus stop in subfreezing weather) are a way to prevent colds when the temperature falls. (It's okay to cut the pom-pom off the hat grandma made if they'll then wear it!)

■ Don't let a simple cold, runny nose or cough go too long without treatment. Two to three days is the maximum any fever should be allowed to "run its course" without treatment by a doctor.

■ Strengthen your heart through aerobic exericse, quit smoking and lose weight if needed.

■ Protect yourself and family from ultraviolet rays. There is no such thing as a "healthy tan" anymore.

■ Try to get adequate amounts of rest. When you are tired and run-down, your body is more susceptible to illness. By taking a hot bath first, you will probably begin to feel more relaxed.

■ Do not allow the kids to talk you into letting a stray, feathery or furry critter stay at your house no matter how cute the animal is.

■ A no-smoking policy in your home will solve the problem of a smoke-allergic reaction. Air cleaners can also help your family avoid bronchial problems.

■ One friend whose son had allergies had an allergist who charged $50 per visit. When her son began his symptoms, the doctor would tell her to bring him in later that day. By the time the appointment arrived, the allergy reaction was out of control. Twice his wheezing and congestion led to a six day-hospital stay. His condition was treated on a reaction basis rather than on the more common-sense preventive-care approach. Her current allergist has a preventive-care style. They schedule in advance two appointments per year and at that time the allergist provides her with medication for emergency use. He manages the asthma by dealing with the signs of trouble right away. At the slightest problem, she calls the doctor and he advises and answers questions over the phone.

■ A respected doctor told me of a situation that is costly and can be avoided. Many patients with hay-fever symptoms ask him to refer them to a specialist. Although he admits that hay fever is frustrating and difficult to control, his opinion is that a specialist is not always necessary. This pediatric endocrinologist told me that severe cases of asthma require powerful medications, frequent hospitalizations, allergy shots and skin testing. However, sneezing and watery eyes attributed to being allergic to household dust, cigarettes, feathery pillows and animals can be treated by avoiding the troublesome objects and hay fever can be controlled by over-the-counter remedies or a prescription.

Remember: Don't be afraid to question a doctor. My sister, a mother of four, offers the following advice, "When a doctor prescribes a medicine that you fear may be expensive, ask if there is a generic brand, which may be less costly but would be just as effective. I have put nearly a hundred extra dollars in my own pocket this year instead of grudgingly passing it over the pharmacy counter."

GOOD GROOMING MONEY-SAVERS

The first step to good grooming is to have clean kids, but sometimes you have to add a little excitement, to pull them away from a favorite activity or television show.

■ Buy a handheld shower massage and let the kids play Niagara Falls as they let the water plunge all over them. By using the shower method for washing and the novelty of a pulsating spray they can regulate, the getting-clean-before-bed mission can be accomplished. This method of production-line washing, by doing several kids in quick succession, not only saves time but money too.

Health related resources:

Herbal Medicine, a book by Dian Dincin Buchman, is chock-full of natural ways to get well and stay healthy.

Buy a family medical guide, preferably one written or edited by the American Medical Association. A complete guide will answer many questions about common diseases, their symptoms and treatments and may help you determine if the illness or ailment is a simple annoyance or a condition that indicates a physician's care is advisable. Consult the following books: *Guide to Your Family's Symptoms* and the *American Medical Association's Family Medical Guide* (Random House), *The Good Housekeeping Family Health and Medical Guide* (Hearst Corporation), *The Complete Guide to Early Child Care*, written by Nicholas Cunningham and the Columbia School of Physicians and Surgeons, Crown Books. Of course, no book should be a substitute for professional medical care.

For a free copy of *Health Hotlines*, a directory of addresses and toll-free numbers of 250 helpful organizations that deal with issues related to asthma, Parkinson's disease, migraine headaches and many others, write to Hotlines, National Library of Medicine Information Office, 8600 Rockville Pike, Bethesda, MD 20894.

Write to the Consumer Information Catalog, P.O. Box 100, Pueblo, CO 81002. Request the Consumer Information Catalog, which offers over two hundred federal publications that are available at little or no cost. These government booklets address exercise, weight control, health, food, nutrition, medical problems, drugs, health aids and much more (highly recommended).

■ When the kids are really sticky and dirty from a day of playing outside, wash them down with the hose on the patio before they come into the house.

■ Before leaving the house for a family party or even a day trip to a park, put a damp washcloth in a plastic bag. Pop it in the glove compartment and use for a quick wipe of the childrens' hands and faces. Also take a squirt bottle filled with water for extra help to "clean up before we get to grandma's." These items are especially handy at a park or playground because the restroom facilities never seem to be in your area.

■ For the kids' hair, I buy the store brand shampoo and dilute it with water, usually 50:50. The less expensive brands work just fine and I don't get upset when the kids use more than the recommended portion — after all, it's half water.

■ Some shampoos and conditioners are premixed in one bottle. Lathering up only once saves time and tears when you can wash hair and remove tangles in one step.

■ Teach the family the proper amount of toothpaste to use so they do not waste it by using more than needed to do the job.

■ Buy colored soap crayons in the drugstore or toy store. My kids "color" on the wall tiles and on the interior of the tub while they play in the bathtub. The beauty of this activity is that they get their whole bodies clean because they draw on themselves. The soap crayons are exactly that, colorful soaps shaped like crayons, designed for creative drawing activity in the bathtub.

■ Save the little slivers of soap and almost-finished bars. Sew a washcloth on three sides. Put the soap in the the three-sided pouch. When the kids wet the washcloth, the soap foams up and bubbles go all over them, getting them clean while they have fun.

■ Put food coloring in the bath water for an occasional surprise. My kids especially love it when I put bubbles in from Ivory or Joy liquid dish detergent (not dishwasher detergent) and add green food coloring so the bubbles are green too.

■ Make your own baby wipes. Place a small amount of baby oil and some soapy water in an empty baby-wipe container. Add folded paper towels to the container and you have your own premoistened minitowels for necessary baby cleanups.

■ Nothing stains worse and ruins more baby outfits than liquid baby vitamins in a dropper bottle. The solution: Administer the drops while babies are in the bathtub — no chance of vitamins staining their clothes then.

■ To save time and reduce laundry, assign each family member his own towel and washcloth in a particular color. Also designate one rack or hook for each person. After bathing, each person is responsible for hanging up towel and cloth in his own spot. This eliminates the habit of each person using a clean towel following each shower, which means less laundry detergent, less electricity for operating the washer and dryer, less time spent folding and putting away and to sum up . . . less work for you.

■ Make a chart that lists such things as brush teeth, get dressed, put away pajamas, make bed . . . get allowance.

■ You can save time and money by trimming the kids' hair yourself. Gather your own tools of the trade: a comb, squirt bottle and good pair of scissors. There are books in the library that show techniques for cutting bangs, giving a blunt cut, or just trimming the ends. A 1977 edition of a book titled *How to Cut Your Own or Anybody Else's Hair* published by Simon and Schuster taught my husband and me the basics.

■ If you are not courageous enough to risk cutting hair, or have tried it once with disastrous results (it eventually grows back!), there are beauty culture schools that will cut and style hair for a reasonable fee. Look in the Yellow Pages and call for hours of operation, services offered and costs. The students enrolled in these schools practice on your lovely locks, and I have never had a bad experience. Beauty culture schools may also offer manicures, pedicures and nail sculpturing, usually for the cost of materials.

■ Keeping boys' hairstyles short makes hair care minimal and presents a tidy, well-groomed look.

■ Some beauty salons charge less for a haircut if your hair is freshly washed that day. If your hair is already clean, you eliminate the step of shampooing, thus you only pay for the time they spend snipping and trimming. If you leave with your hair still wet from their squirt bottle, that might eliminate the blow-dry styling charge.

■ If you just need a simple cut, a barbershop may cost less than a salon.

■ In our neighborhood, a mother of five and former hairdresser cuts hair at her home. She does a great job with perms, haircuts and haircoloring processes. The price is reasonable, and you don't have those dreadful long waits often experienced at pricey salons. Is there a former hairdresser in your neighborhood? Check grocery store bulletin boards for people offering these services. If you have a service to offer, consider bartering haircuts for mending or occasional babysitting.

■ My hairdresser filled me in on a beauty supply store that is open to the public. It costs a lot less to buy concentrated bottles of shampoo and add your own water. The store sells a great variety of cosmetics, too.

There seems to be an ongoing discussion over the issue of disposable versus cloth diapers. The disposables average between twenty and thirty cents each depending on the brand and the size. A baby or toddler can go through about ten a day, which adds up to two or three dollars' worth. Thirty days in a month times a ballpark figure of $2.50 is approximately $75 monthly. This amount multiplied by twelve months is almost a thousand dollars. Multiply that times two-and-a-half years of diapering per child.

The calculations for cloth diapers are — ten cloth diapers times one dollar each equals ten dollars. The diapers last for a couple of years. Add the cost of electricity to run the washer and dryer, the detergent and the bleach, and cloth diapers may still cost much less. But there is the hygiene issue to consider, especially in a day-care environment when diapering is a routine. Cloth diapers must be cleaned and sanitized or they can spread disease. The convenience of disposable diapers cannot be disputed and degradable disposable diapers are making their marketing debut. Using coupons for disposable diapers is a money-saving opportunity and I find the generic brands to be adequate. You might use cloth diapers at home and disposables when you are out and need convenience.

Home Remedies

Natural beauty recipes range from conditioning shampoos to toothpaste.

■ When you want to get back to basics and feel rather brave, try combining 2 tablespoons of baking soda with 2 tablespoons of powdered cinnamon and 2 tablespoons oil of cinnamon. My 91-year-old uncle swears by this recipe for toothpaste.

■ If you grew up in the 1950s you probably remember your grandmother using a well-beaten egg blended with shampoo for her version of a conditioning formula to give hair extra shine and body. Another version is a mixture of 2 cups of liquid castile soap, one-half cup of olive oil and 1 cup of distilled water. Shake it in an empty shampoo bottle, and voilà — homemade shampoo. (I prefer almond oil in place of olive oil for a nice scent. Try your health food store for almond oil.)

■ Is there an alternative to commercial dandruff shampoos? Yes, if you believe my elderly relative. "Just brew up some sage tea and rinse your hair."

■ People in my grandmother's day used cornstarch instead of baby powder. A friend told me that she stretches the quantity of store-brand baby powder by combining half name-brand or store-brand and half cornstarch from a grocery store. The generic brand of baby shampoo is great, too.

Keeping your kids healthy and well-groomed seems like a lot of work but since your family's health is your first million dollars, I am in favor of protecting my most precious assets by being vigilant about health care. Implementing the health and grooming tips in this chapter will pay off splendidly, too.

CHAPTER FIVE

Entertaining Your Kids

E ntertaining your kids may sound a bit refined for most harried parents; we simply want ideas for fun-raising with the family that will allow us to step down from the treadmill for at least a few hours. Whining choruses of "Can you play with me? Let's go for a ride," and "I'm so bored" seem to begin before the end of the weekend's first cartoon show or a mere five hours into summer vacation. We often forget to let kids know that the time we spend with them is valued. Unfortunately, the demands of career, family and chores detract from quality family time. It seems nearly impossible to schedule outings and activities that can create a close family bond without putting yourself in the poorhouse. However, with a little ingenuity, there are lots of low-cost ways to put your worries behind, at least for a while, and really have some fun with your kids.

Writing this chapter has given me the opportunity to share my friends' and neighbors' ideas. Use them as a tool to spark your imagination and as a source of inspiration. Add your own personal touch to these ideas for getting back to nature and experiencing another culture. We considered costs of all activities because most families are on tight budgets. Our activities are low- or no-expense, yet lots of fun. You will find that everyday materials used in a slightly different manner will open exciting ideas for family fun.

Let's begin with some ways to keep everyone creatively entertained when the weather outside indicates it is a stay-at-home kind of day.

INDOOR FUN

Rainy days, snowy days . . . days that the kids don't know what to do with themselves. "Can I invite a friend over?" or "Can you drive me to Anna's house?" are innocent questions, but it is easier on you if you have some ideas stashed away for days such as these. Keep a trinket box handy on the top shelf of a closet with "to-the-rescue-boredom-buster" materials already prepared. Or, try some of these for lasting fun.

Bring Back the Memories Box

Tucked away inside the "baby box" you stored are memories that will bring many moments of happiness for you and the kids. They love looking at their baby clothes, locks of hair, birth certificate, hospital baby pictures, plastic identification bracelet and that first footprint. (Try bringing to mind that little crescent shape with the tiny circle toes the next time you are scrubbing fingerprints off the living-room wall.) Describe the house where you lived when they were first born, who came to goo and gaa at them in the hospital, and tell stories about them when they were babies. If practical, take a ride to visit the hospital where they were born. Go into the coffee shop, have a soda and talk about how excited you were as you bundled them up and left for the trip home with your new baby. Point out the special things about the hospital like the gift shop and maternity ward. We tape recorded those early cries of our kids, when they first cooed and first talked on the telephone. They love replaying their own priceless early-years cassette tape. This would be an unusual twist to celebrate each birthday—bring out the baby box. (Do this as an age-appropriate activity; there is a certain age where all of this becomes embarrassing to a kid. Then, put it away for appreciation in years to come when it all becomes enchanting again.)

At the very least, you could just get cozy on the couch and look through a box of old photographs or some picture albums.

Treasure Hunt

Give one child some old jewelry, paper clips, stickers, pennies, wrapped candy, pieces of gum, hair clips or trinkets to hide inside your house. The other kids, the "finders" count to fifty with your help or if they are too young to count, sing "Happy Birthday" three times. You can also keep them occupied while the "hider" is hiding by providing paper and markers and help to draw a map of your home. The one who did the hiding gives clues to help others find the hidden objects. Set a goal such as trying to find all of the treasures before a song on the record player is finished playing.

Fashion Show

Bring out the old sport outfits, Halloween costumes, wigs, makeup, fake beards, jewelry, coats, gowns, hats, formal wear, ballerina outfits and other outlandish garments. Encourage the children to create their fantasies or act out a favorite television character. Turn your radio to a soft FM station or play a tape for background music. You can be the narrator as the kids strut their stuff and really get into the spirit of a living-room show.

Quick and Easy Popsicles

Frozen yogurt, pudding pops, watermelon treats and juice Popsicles can be made quickly and without much mess. When you have a few minutes, freeze some liquids such as lemonade, flavored Kool-Aid and grape juice in an extra ice cube tray or a Popsicle mold to make some treats for your family. My kids love to make gelatin and freeze it in ice cube trays. For a party, add the gelatin ice cubes to the punch. Or put the liquids in paper cups and freeze. They become push-up juice ices when frozen. Try mixing one cup of fruit juice and one cup of canned or fresh fruit in a blender. Put it in paper cups to freeze. If you have popsicle sticks or plastic spoons, put them in when the mixture starts to feel firm or about half-frozen. Continue to freeze.

Another favorite treat is frozen yogurt. Blend a sliced banana, one teaspoon of vanilla, fruit chunks and one cup of plain yogurt in the blender. Pour in small paper cups and freeze. To make watermelon treats, blend seedless watermelon chunks with unsweetened orange juice and water (use equal portions of all three ingredients). Freeze in small paper cups.

Did you ever freeze green grapes? What a great treat! They are so sweet, better-tasting than candy.

Hocus-Pocus Magic Time

There are many easy tricks using coins and cards for aspiring magicians to learn. Borrow some books from the library and help your child master a few "presto chango" tricks. Don't forget the old faithfuls such as rubbing a balloon against a wool sweater and magically sticking it to the wall or magnets mysteriously picking up metallic household objects. Fashion a black cape from a piece of fabric or an old skirt, and make a magic wand. Practice a few times with your child and get ready to beam with pride the first time your young magician entertains.

Here are some ideas for fun that are low cost and easy to do:

■ Make paper chains. Make lots of paper decorations with construction paper and odds and ends.

■ Redecorate your kitchen for a special day called "red day." Have a red snack, tell the story of Little Red Riding Hood, hide items that are red for the children to look for.

■ Make cookie houses out of graham crackers using frosting to glue them together. Decorate with tiny candies, raisins, licorice, cookies, coconut and pieces of dried fruit.

■ Put some candy sprinkles in a shaker bottle and let the kids decorate store-bought cakes or cookies. Frosting for the cookies and a few toppings are all they need to have fun.

■ Make a collage out of colored cupcake papers.

■ Make a train with your kitchen chairs lined up in a row. Tear up pieces of paper for tickets.

■ Make a hopscotch game on the back of an old vinyl tablecloth for an indoor game of hopscotch. Play on the kitchen floor.

■ Give the child three or four household items. Make up or act out a story using those items.

■ Draw your own comic strip. Make up a superhero and give the hero magical powers.

■ Make an obstacle course by having children go around a chair, crawl under a table, knock three times on a door, jump over a throw rug, etc.

■ Empty two-liter soda bottles (small juice cans, empty detergent bottles, potato chip cylinders with lids, etc.) make great bowling pins. Add a little sand or some pebbles to the bottles to make them more stable, and use a soft ball or lightweight playground ball as a bowling ball (best in the basement or a clear area such as on the kitchen floor).

■ Hang crepe paper streamers vertically from the top of a door in the kitchen to create a stage effect. Children love to peak through to sing songs, act out a play or put on a puppet show.

■ Soak rice or uncooked macaroni in water tinted with food coloring. Remove when colored. After drying, use it to make collages on paper or wood. (Cover a section with glue, pour on colored rice or pasta and dump off the extra.)

■ Buy a large bag of already-popped popcorn and let the children build interesting structures by using toothpicks to connect one piece to the other.

■ Teach the kids to sew. A scrap bag of material and buttons along with needles and colored thread can provide hours of fun.

■ Let them play in the bathtub. Color the water with food coloring. To make bubbles, add liquid dish detergent such as Joy.

■ Get children in the spirit of collecting their old toys, books and clothes for a future flea market or garage sale. Tell them that they can keep 50 percent of the profits if they help clear out the closets.

Don't forget the old standbys of building blocks; puzzles; playing store or hairdresser; listening to music; paint-by-water books; building a tent under a table; making a mask with paper plates, cardboard, brown paper bags and cereal boxes; coloring; reading stories; finger painting; colored chalk; water play in the sink; board games and clay. And if you are really feeling energetic, you can make papier-mâché, modeling clay, paste or sugar cookies. Check craft books at the library for easy recipes.

OUTDOOR FUN

There is a giant, wondrous world outside and lots of energy inside. Take time to get outside with the kids. The fresh air will do you good, the kids will get the exercise they need and may even come home complacent and, without any prodding from you, straighten up their rooms (no guarantees on that!).

Open the door and explore places and ideas that can turn everyday surroundings into new adventures.

Scavenger Hunt

If you live near any kind of water—ocean, lake or pond—you can spend the day exploring with a purpose. Before you arrive, make a list of the items that each child must find. Don't make the list too easy or your hunt will be over too quickly. Each child needs a sack. In addition to things that each one collects, list things that they can observe and check off on their list. Be specific when you list the type of shell, seaweed, bird, feather, fish or the color of sand that you want them to notice. Add a mother with a baby, a kite, a person with a fishing net, a mushroom, pinecone or a child wearing something yellow to your list of observations.

You could adapt this activity to be a Forest Scavenger Hunt by simply changing the items collected or noticed. For the backyard, give each child a lunch bag and have them look for tree bark, a vegetable, a feather, clover, a round stone, a bug, a blossom, a sprout, weeds, roots, a walking stick, etc.

Feed the Creatures—Go Animal Watching!

Not enough time to go to a zoo? Just raid your refrigerator and cabinets for crumbs and stale pieces of bread. Pack them in a brown lunch bag. Take a walk around the neighborhood and feed whatever little creatures you see. If you have a few extra minutes, go to a nearby pond and feed the ducks and birds. Have a contest to see who can see the most squirrels, nests or pigeons.

Try these ideas for more outside fun:

■ Make a bird feeder by spreading honey on a pinecone and then rolling the pinecone in cereal or birdseed. Twist a piece of wire around the top to form a loop so you can hang the cone treat from a tree.

■ When you have table scraps such as rice, cheese or spaghetti, give them to the birds to enjoy. (Put the food on the bird ledge of a feeder, not on the ground, and only during cold weather. Uninvited guests, such as ants, will visit otherwise.)

■ Go out early and listen to the sounds of nature before the rest of the world comes alive.

■ Collect wildflowers and ferns in the woods.

■ Observe the stars, watch the clouds and gaze at the sky.

■ Plant a tree.

■ Pick up litter.

■ Go bird-watching. Scatter crumbs, sunflower seeds, fruit bits and bird food.

■ Make a cake for the birds by mixing 1 cup peanut butter, 2 cups bird seed, 5 cups cornmeal, and 1 cup melted beef suet. Put in a paper-lined cupcake tin in the refrigerator until cooled. Save mesh bags (the kind that oranges, grapefruit and onions come in) and empty the birds' cakes into bags. Hang on a tree for the birds' snack.

FUN AROUND THE TOWN

There are those glorious times when your life does appear to be in order. Family matters have fallen neatly in place and you have time to play. You may even have a few extra dollars in your pocket! Family field trips or day trips allow you and the children to view the environment and explore the community as well as provide new windows of discovery and wonder. Don't forget your camera, and why not tape-record the kids sharing their experiences when they come home from sight-seeing or feeding the birds?

An Elegant Morning Out

Sometimes even when money is tight, it is fun to splurge on nonessentials, such as a pot of tea and scones. Two mothers I know dressed their children in their "Sunday Best" clothes and gave them a crash course on fine restaurant etiquette. They made reservations for tea in an English Tea Room. Everyone acted so proper, and the children felt grown up as they were seated at their own table and ordered for themselves. They thrived on acting like they did this regularly. Just a slight change of routine but it did wonders for the mothers emotionally, too.

Spectator Sportwatching

My children have yet to actually play soccer (they are involved in other activities), but we have logged hundreds of hours watching the community teams practice on Friday nights at our local recreation center. The light of the moon and the bright lights on the field make it a fun way to spend an evening. The lure of the swings and sliding board on the adjacent field has provided many hours of fun after dark as the lights for the sporting event illuminate the playground. Signing your kids up for sport activities is a great experience for them and a good investment for you. Lots of lessons are learned early on the playing field.

When the weather is too cold to play outside, head for a local ski resort and sit in the ski lodge with the kids. There is plenty of action and excitement watching people of all ages ski down the slopes. Sipping hot chocolate and being warmed by the fire at a ski resort is a nice place to be when the windchill factor outside reaches 25 degrees below zero.

If a ski resort isn't close, consider these other ideas:

- Take the kids to watch another sport in action. Bundle up with sweaters and coats and don your ski masks, gloves and boots. For comfort, bring your own jug of something warm to drink.
- Drive to the top of a ridge and watch the snowmobilers, sledders and cross-country skiers from the comfort of your car.
- When the lake freezes over, watch the older kids play ice hockey.
- Watch the speed skaters practice at an indoor or outdoor rink.

Music Appreciation

If you want your children to cultivate a lifelong love affair with music, take them to rehearsals for the university orchestra or ballet and recitals by music students. Check the small weekly papers or the entertainment section to see if these concerts are available. Call ahead for permission, or sneak in as quiet as a mouse. It goes without saying, babies and toddlers are not included for this family outing. Many communities offer free concerts in the park during the summer. Take a blanket and enjoy. In the park's informal atmosphere, the kids can even get up and dance.

Poor Person's Tour of the City

Major historical societies are justifiably proud of the city's most interesting historical buildings and sights. Unfortunately, the costs of these tours are out of reach for many parents with children. So, for the price of a bus ticket, you can take a ride around the city pointing out places of interest to your kids. You are probably already familiar with the area from your own childhood, but a quick trip to the library could give you information about any free museums or exhibits. Find out about the landmarks, statues, fountains and the scenic wonders all around you.

Grocery Shopping — Fun?

Many times food shopping seems like one more burden that parents could live without. Kids are often tired and whiny while you attempt to shop for weekly necessities, trying to remember the essentials on your list that was accidentally left on the kitchen table when you answered the phone. A new attitude may be just what you need to make this errand enjoyable. Involve the older child (notice not more than one!) in the selection of goods. Make it a game, like a treasure hunt. Present the child with a coupon for a needed item and let the child search the store for it. Not only is it a help in that you remember to use your coupons, but it is a wonderful reading-skill activity, even for older children who must check expiration dates and find appropriate product sizes. Start the younger children with cereal and cookie coupons. You'll be amazed at their product recognition. Give the older kids a calculator and have them keep track of the price of items they are responsible for choosing. This activity teaches them analysis, reading and even something about spending.

Afternoon at the Holiday Inn

Kids will love this idea, although at first you may think it is unlikely that it could be fun. Try it, you'll see. Visit a high-rise hotel and take the kids for a ride on the glass elevator that overlooks the lobby below. Go to the top floor and gaze out at the city below. A no-cost panoramic view awaits you and the children as you observe the hustle and bustle of city life. Bring along a few extra quarters so you can visit the game room. Some hotels have skating and swimming facilities that are open to the public for a minimal fee.

Flea Market Finds

Garage sales and flea markets abound on the weekend. Give each child two dollars that can be spent for any purpose. No input from parents allowed. Resist the temptation to say, "We don't need anymore junk around the house." Let them walk around and search for those unbelievable bargains on which to spend that wonderful money.

"U"-Pick Farms

Probably right in your own neighborhood or within a short drive, there is some kind of growing going on. Picking your own fruits and vegetables, such as blueberries, lima beans, peaches, asparagus, pumpkins and apples at a produce farm or orchard is a great way to have some fun with the kids. When you return home, bake a special treat with your fresh-picked goodies. Pack a picnic lunch before you go in order to sit in a field and experience the true feeling of eating in Farmer McGregor's garden, just like Peter Rabbit. Since the growing seasons of vegetables vary, it is best to call ahead for hours of operation. Check your local newspapers, the Yellow Pages and ask around.

FUN WITH RELATIVES

Getting together with relatives is fun. In addition to the usual chatting and snacking that is the cornerstone of family parties, here are some ways to add extra pizzazz to gatherings. Included are new ways to create memories, both inside and outside of the home, and a few suggestions for enriching memories with your own children. I know many people do not live near relatives. People whose relatives live across the country or state are usually resourceful and have established a network of friends that are "almost family." Why not improvise by reaching out to friends, church members and "significant others" to join you for some modified family activities?

Make a Family Tree Party

Invite lots of relatives over for a nostalgic evening in which memories are shared. Gather stories from the grandparents about the olden days and record them on audio, video or paper. Ask each person to bring an item such as an album, an old quilt, a handicraft, a scrapbook, a box of letters and pictures. Memories of parents, grandparents and great-grandparents make great stories. Talk about the people in the old pictures and begin to draw a family tree. Perhaps a relative has duplicate pictures of someone or an event that holds much sentimental value for another relative. Swaps and gifts of such photos could be arranged.

Intergenerational History Lesson

Invite an elderly relative to take a bus or car ride with you and the kids. They will be thrilled to point out the area's hot spots from their early days, and may even be able to recount the history behind the old firehouse or the stadium.

Take the kids along with an older relative to the Historical Society. Look at the exhibits and pictures. Observe how the town looked a hundred years ago. Find out who owned the land where you live now. Did they have children who played in your yard? What were the kids' names? What landmarks can you visit? Ask your relative to tell you more about this period of local history.

Grandparents Night

Invite the grandparents over for a little program to honor them. The children can prepare by making cheerful decorations, putting on a little play or musical show and giving them homemade cards that say how much they love them. Simple snacks made by the kids are served. Ask grandpa if he can show any magic tricks that he learned as a kid. Ask grandma to bring a special recipe that she enjoyed making with her kids, and offer to help her make it.

What's Different?

We remember when candy bars were only twelve cents and computers, Nintendos and microwave ovens were nonexistent. Elderly relatives can delve back into their past and share what it was like without televisions and cars. Kids will be amazed when grandpa relates that he had to work to support the family and he was only a kid himself. What was school like in those days? How were you taught? What did you learn? Compare the kinds of food we eat now — fast-food drive-thrus vs. family sit-down roast beef dinners that were a tradition every Sunday.

And the Band Plays On

Does your uncle still have his harmonica? What instruments do your kids play? If you come from a musical family, let everyone do a solo performance and then play together just for fun. But if you are like our family, the family band is a fancy name for a collection of flowerpots, pans, juice cans, and upside-down wastebaskets gathered to create our own unique sounds. Use pencils or spoons to tap or bang along to the beat of the music. Drinking glasses filled with different amounts of water make pleasant musical sounds. We have fun singing the words to old favorites like "Yankee Doodle" and "Oh! Susannah" while humming, strumming and singing aloud.

That Was Then! This Is Now!

Gather pictures of you when you were your child's age and place them side-by-side next to current pictures of your child. Are you similar in appearance? How are you different? Share the high points you remember about friends and activities you enjoyed. Tell stories about your brothers, sisters and family vacations. (They love to hear the war stories about when you got into trouble.)

Nostalgia Night

It is so much fun to look back and remember with the aid of photographs, newspaper clippings and old home movies. When was the last time you took the kids on a ride to see the house where you grew up or took them to play at your favorite playground? Visit the neighborhood where they were born. Stop by and say hello to someone who hasn't seen your family in years. Visit the neighborhood store where the elderly butcher might say, "I knew your mom and dad when they were your age." Think about the things you have stored away in that old chest — your diary, school photos, scout uniform and old report cards. The kids will be in heaven as they dress up in your wedding gown or play with your yo-yo. *Warning:* Once they know about your nostalgia box, it will become one of their favorite pastimes. Keep it locked securely if you don't want them to take your teenage love letters in to their teacher for show-and-tell or to read hysterically to their friends on the school bus.

LOW-COST IDEAS FOR PARTIES AND NEIGHBORHOOD GET-TOGETHERS

Although the ideas in this section are intended for family fun, they can be easily adapted as themes for birthday parties or neighborhood get-togethers that are low cost and quite enjoyable.

Visit America First

This activity begins when the parents and kids get together and select a few places they would like to visit. This doesn't have to get complicated and actually the simpler the better. We have a rich heritage of foods in the United States. Both children and adults enjoy tasting and learning about unusual foods from other parts of the country. For breakfast, make sourdough pancakes, a favorite in Alaska and other western states. A southwestern favorite, such as chili con carne, can be prepared for lunch, and from the cookbooks of Wyoming come Sheridan Cow Belle Beefburgers, which are hearty favorites among the ranchers and sheep growers. Think of a theme for your day, such as a rodeo, and let everyone get into the spirit with cowboy attire or scarves tied around their necks. (This idea could also be adapted with an international flair for foreign countries.)

Out-of-This-World Sandwich-Making Party

Announce to your friends and family that Saturday's lunch will be served at your house at noon. Each child is to bring the ingredients to "assemble" or "construct" a sandwich — but not just any mere sandwich or hoagie. The kids are going to be using their imagination to create a space-age sandwich. Moms and dads should send along things like alfalfa sprouts, olives, french bread, round rolls, onions, pickles, cold cuts, grated cheese, shredded lettuce and sliced tomatoes. Space ships, flying saucers, rocket ships, constellations, space creatures and all kinds of "out-of-this-world" sandwiches were created by our neighborhood kids. They were fun to make and eat. Just give them the ingredients and they will amaze you with the designs they come up with. No instruction from adults is necessary.

Quick-and-Easy Pet Show Party

Not everyone has a real pet, but what child doesn't own a favorite stuffed animal? Lions, tigers and stuffed bears are all invited to the First Annual Neighborhood Pet Show. Prizes are awarded to participants for the following categories — most affectionate, best watch-pet, friendliest, most eager to please, most alert, best disposition, oldest, etc. Large boxes, felt-tipped markers, string, construction paper scraps, fabric pieces and crayons are needed so the kids can decorate cages that are joined together for a living-room circus train. Animal crackers add to the theme.

Make-Your-Own-Movie Night

Invite the neighborhood kids over for a movie and popcorn party. This can be a spur-of-the-moment event or one that is planned in advance. Gather the props (gloves, cup, typewriter, ball, wig, rake, old jacket, etc.) from around your house and place them in a basket. Give the aspiring actors some time to make up a script using the objects you have collected from around the house. Get that movie camera rolling so you can record the live talent. Play the movie back for them and serve buttered popcorn to the filmmakers, amateur producers and stars. Have an early evening showing for the parents. The kids can bring a comforter and pillow and have a minisleepover. The parents can watch the movie, socialize and enjoy popcorn.

"Come as a Song" Party

Friends and family receive a cleverly crafted invitation that invites them to a party where they must dress up as a song. You will be surprised at how enthused people are to go along with this theme. Some of our guests came as "The Purple People Eater," a huge refrigerator-box creation painted purple, naturally, and containing family members within. Another family dressed as a box of Crayola crayons in celebration of the "Color My World" song. We had a six-foot "Frosty the Snowman," even though we held the event in the sweltering heat of June. We videotaped each family singing their song, and then sat back and watched the special event over and over again. Sing-alongs are a great low-cost activity.

Neighborhood Campfire

In our neighborhood, which consists of fifteen homes, we hold an annual fall hayride, followed by an old-fashioned "wienie roast" in a volunteer's backyard. One of the neighbors hooks a cart to the back of the lawn tractor that is filled with hay. The kids take turns going around the cul-de-sac in the hay cart. The event begins at dusk and continues until around 10 P.M. Each family brings hot dogs, rolls and a dessert to share with the group. Even if you can't have a hayride, how about a campfire in someone's backyard? Neighbors can pool their musical abilities and have a sing-along.

Game Night

Invite the neighbors over for a night of game activities. Concentration, Trivial Pursuit, Candy Land, Bingo, Cootie, Dominoes, Checkers and Boggle are fun for all. After a few hours of board games, you could try word games, card games (Old Maid, Rummy, Fish, Snap, Hearts, Crazy Eights and War), quiz games or charades. Some enjoyable outdoor games are Red Rover, horseshoes, balloon volleyball, relay races, croquet, hopscotch, jump rope and a scavenger hunt. If you get a burst of energy and creativity, invent a new game together or change the rules of a board game to make it different. Here are some variations: use two colors of mint candies for checkers or M&M's for Monopoly houses and motels. Every time you pass "go," you collect five pieces of candy. Use soda bottle caps and buttons for markers. Use real money in place of game money. Pennies, nickels, dimes and quarters have inflated values in the new rules game!

Tasting Party

Tired of serving the same old foods? Why not introduce new food ideas by having a tasting party? Sample different fruits, cheeses or cereals. Include three or four kinds and compare colors, tastes and appearances.

One group of parents scheduled Friday nights as Potluck Dinner night (and in warm weather, a potluck picnic). Nothing fancy, but each family brings a favorite dish.

Exotic Foreign Parties

Hawaiian. Take your family to Hawaii by bringing out the flowered shirts, paper leis, seashells and colorful grass skirts that can be fashioned with things you have around the house. Ask your local travel agent for a scenic poster or two to help create a relaxing Hawaiian atmosphere. Set up your beach umbrella and bring out the colorful beach towels. Go through the motions of a long plane ride or a fun boat ride across the Pacific. Play a Hawaiian record borrowed from the library and videotape the kids doing a Hawaiian dance. Enjoy a feast with a buffet of fruits, shish kebabs and sweet-and-sour pork. Sample the flavor of coconuts, pineapples, bananas and mangos. A sensory obstacle course could be set up to simulate the barefoot feeling of Hawaii. Walk through a box of sand, dip your toes in a basin of water, walk over some smooth stones, etc. Invite some friends over to make fish-shaped cookies to be decorated with lots of beautiful colors to look like the tropical fish found in Hawaii. Drink Hawaiian Punch, of course!

Mexican. Make your own tacos, piñatas, masks, flowers and merry Mexican music (borrow Mexican records from the library). These are just a few of the ways to have a fiesta with your *amigos* Mexican-style. Since Mexico is a very close neighbor, you may be able to find a Spanish-speaking guest to teach you a few words and show you some traditional games. Find out about their holiday celebrations such as Cinco de Mayo and customs. This can be varied to suit any culture.

Annual Block Party

This requires a planning meeting before the actual event. Everyone pitches in to make this one of the best times of the year. A menu is decided on and each family contributes about $20 to cover the costs of the meat, drinks and paper products, which are bulk-purchased. Everyone contributes a dish to share. We plan games for all of the kids, have a decorated bicycle parade in the early afternoon and a community softball game at 5 P.M. The evening usually winds down with someone playing all of the "oldies," and there is lots of dancing in the front yards of the adjoining properties.

Roaring Twenties

Ask your friends and relatives to dig in their attics to find long beads, felt hats and pleated skirts. Arrange hairstyles to re-create the styles of that glamorous period. Play music and do the dances from the twenties. With information you find at the library, make up a trivia contest. The older folks will light up as they share the fads and events of their young lives. Tape-record their memories as they reminisce about the good old days.

Oldies But Goodies

Moms and Dads get out their old long-playing records of the Beach Boys and Beatles, and play them for the kids (try to resist the temptation to add "Now this was really music!"). It's amazing that we still know all of the words to these songs

F or books filled with specific party tips, menus, games and favors for childrens' parties, I recommend:

Birthday Parties by Vicki Lansky, 18326 Minnetonka Blvd. PG, Deephaven, MN 55391 ($9.95).

How to Entertain Children at Home or in Preschool, also highly recommended, is chock-full of ideas for year-round fun, games, projects, arts-and-crafts experiences, songs, activities and places to go for free supplies. Available for purchase by sending $14.95 to *Child Care Ideas*, Box 442, King of Prussia, PA 19406.

Also available are valuable idea-filled special reports for indoor and outdoor activities, *100 Ways to Keep Kids Happy, Cook Up Some Fun With the Kids, Nature and More . . . Let's Explore* and *Get Up and Go With Your Kids: A Parent's Survival Guide* ($3 each).

while we have long-since forgotten the state capitals. And it is still a lot of fun to sing and act out the lyrics. The old feelings just seem to come back as the old folks (the "thirty-somethings") get up and do a stomp or line dance. Remember wearing your hair in a flip and the popularity of tattered jeans? The kids will love hearing all about it and after they are done hysterically laughing on the floor, they will try to imitate the dancing steps, too!

Pan American Games

Games are a good way for people to get to know each other. They are also a lot of fun when feelings aren't hurt and everyone is included. Talk to people who were born in other countries and inquire about the games played at parties or in the school recess yards in their homelands. You will learn variations for our games of tag, kickball and jacks. (I just played freeze tag with my kids the other night. I had forgotten how much fun it is to be a kid. You have to be thick-skinned when you realize your third-grader can run faster than you.)

HOLIDAY ACTIVITIES

Everyone has memories of special family traditions. Most parents want to share the delights of their own early years with their children. These recollections serve as a starting point for the traditions we have preserved for our own little ones. The excitement of receiving greeting cards, making our own artistic creations, opening packages and decorating for a special celebration are clearly remembered and suddenly we are like little children again. Traditions are important for children and for you, too. Ask your friends, both near and far, how they celebrate with their families.

Christmas

As kids, we made cookies using an old family recipe. This was another special activity of which a wonderful part (besides the fun of baking together) was always sharing our festive fixings with someone in need. We also made "hidden special treasure" cupcakes. Mom hid "a Christmas surprise" in one cupcake before baking.

■ For the thirty days before Christmas, have each person take a holiday decoration out of the box and hang it up. Little by little, wreaths, mistletoe, candy canes, candles and the pinecone centerpiece contribute to a festive glow for the house.

■ Decorate the inside of windows with Christmas scenes by using white shoe polish — the kind that comes with an applicator. It is not messy and wipes right off after the holiday with a damp rag or sponge.

■ Send a family holiday letter telling friends and relatives news of the year.

■ Window-shop in a town you've never visited before.

■ Listen to the music of a holiday concert at a church, college or mall. These concerts are listed in the newspaper calendar of events.

■ Host a "trim-the-tree party." String popcorn and cranberries. Or gather simple supplies in advance and host a "make-a-Christmas-ornament" party. The host family serves Christmas punch, cookies and the invited families bring snacks to share. Punch Recipe: 2 large bottles of ginger ale, 1 can of Hawaiian Punch, 1 large can of orange punch and 1 small bottle of ReaLemon, 6 packages of red Kool-Aid, 2 gallons water, 8 cups sugar.

■ Keep a file throughout the year of ideas you see in magazines or hear about from friends. The ideas can include Christmas party ideas, recipes, simple holiday crafts and easy-to-make decorations.

■ Make the simple craft ideas you see in the womens' magazines, such as winding twine around a juice can or coffee can. Glue pictures from magazines, colored paper and stickers to the can for a colorful collage. Make a star for the top and fill with mints, peanuts, colored popcorn, a granola snack or homemade peanut brittle. Or use the decorated container for a pencil holder, clutter organizer or to store loose change or art supplies.

■ Make photo Christmas ornaments each year using the annual school photographs. Just glue the photo to a regular Christmas ball, add some glitter and mark the date.

■ Create your own greeting cards from magazine cutouts or last year's cards.

■ Compile a Family Christmas Book. Ask relatives to send you their favorite ideas for preparing for Christmas, sharing memories and their most-loved recipes. Ask for short original stories, anecdotes and poems. Type up and make copies at the quick-print shop for each family.

■ Ask an elderly relative or a nursing-home resident what made their family's special events memorable.

■ Blend ideas from your past with fun traditions from around the world. Holiday celebrations unique to other parts of the world can be used to merge cultures.

■ Visit the library and take out books on foreign folklore, poetry and activities. Be sure to learn holiday greetings and terms of endearment as spoken in different languages. Research the origins of holiday symbols and traditions. Ask your international friends to share customs that mark their special days.

■ Buy blank audiotapes and tape some Christmas music from the special holiday programs or from records you borrow from the library.

■ Learn about food, games and exotic legends, and listen to songs from other countries.

■ Act out a nativity scene with your family or stage a Christmas play.

■ Have a birthday party for baby Jesus — complete with cake, candles and singing.

■ Invite neighbors to go Christmas caroling.

■ Change the idea of Christmas from receiving to giving by visiting a nursing home or volunteering to help at a homeless shelter.

■ Spend some time discussing what you feel each family member would truly enjoy.

■ Start a tradition of reading the same Christmas story or watching the same Christmas movie as a family.

■ Have a cookie exchange. Each friend brings a batch of favorite cookies (and the recipe written down on an index card). The cookies are displayed on the dining room table and are distributed equally. Each person has a variety to take home.

■ Have a holiday open house a few days before Christmas. Serve "munchies," eggnog, cheese, crackers and pretzels. Neighbors and friends are invited to stop by for some holiday cheer.

■ Shop the holiday bazaars on the final day, during the final hours when many of the craft tables and baked-good tables have reduced their crafts and goodies by half. Great time to buy baked goods to freeze for unexpected company or to give as gifts.

■ Make the extra effort to celebrate holidays with family traditions. They serve to strengthen the family bond.

Gifts. Use some special time with your child to make gifts for others — twice-blessed benefits!

■ Giant gift cookies are fun to make and challenge the imagination. Use cookie patterns from a store or design your own. Use ornamental frosting to artfully decorate the cookies. Sprinkle colored sugar and use string licorice, gumdrops, raisins to make faces. Wrap each individually with clear plastic. Everyone likes a gift of cookies.

■ Take a homemade present to someone in need or lonely. A few cookies in a plastic bag tied with a colorful ribbon is all it takes to brighten someone's day.

■ Use green and red balloons, cookie cutters, decorated pinecones, jump-rope or household gadgets instead of bows for a present.

■ Make your own gift cards by gluing scraps of wrapping paper to stiff cardboard or construction paper. Fold over and write your message inside. The gift card can match your wrapping paper.

■ Save old Christmas cards to cut down for this year's gift tags. Cutting with pinking shears adds a nice effect.

■ Send children inexpensive storybooks instead of cards. Since the cost of a special Christmas greeting card can be $1.00 to $1.50, this is a more used and appreciated gift/card.

■ Wrap gifts with shelf paper, butcher paper, fabric remnants, newspaper comics, an old calendar, a map or newsprint rubber-stamped with holiday designs. To rubber stamp, cut a sponge into the shape of stars, moon, reindeer, Christmas tree, dip it in paint, squeeze out the excess, and press onto surface to imprint.

■ On blank butcher paper or newsroll paper, write riddles, jokes and recipes for a unique wrapping paper idea.

Halloween

There are alternatives to candy bars as Halloween treats and store-bought costumes as the mode of dress. Try some of these ideas when Halloweening on a budget. But remember, the following treats should be used only for parties or gatherings of friends; they are not appropriate for door-to-door trick-or-treating because of safety reasons.

■ Give out individual packages of hot chocolate mix, pencils or chocolate-flavored straws instead of candy.

■ Serve a cup of hot apple cider and a cookie to the trick-or-treaters. To make: Heat unsweetened apple juice in a pan. Add unsweetened orange juice to suit your taste. Add a cinnamon stick. Simmer for five minutes.

■ Wrap candy corn and popcorn in a napkin. Gather and tie with a thin orange and black ribbon curled up with scissors.

■ Give out chocolate cupcakes or iced brownies decorated with orange frosting and jimmies.

■ Wrap some "trail mix" in individual plastic bags: equal portions of raisins, peanuts, M&M's and tiny pretzels.

■ Make homemade butter cookies, cut out with pumpkin-shaped cookie cutters, and add orange sprinkles.

■ Make up bags of popcorn and wrap in cellophane with orange and black yarn or ribbon (a nutritious snack for the lunchbox the next day). Some people mix plain popcorn with a tiny bit of cinnamon in a plastic bag. Shake and taste. If it passes your own kids' critical taste test, serve to the trick-or-treaters.

■ Make a batch of chocolate-covered pretzels or pretzel rods. At the craft store, they sell "chocolate" in a variety of colors: white, pink, yellow, orange, brown. Melt the chocolate and half-fill a tall glass. Dip the pretzel rod in to coat, roll in orange sprinkles. Or melt the chocolate and put in pumpkin-shaped candy molds that are available at craft stores. They also sell taffy sticks to insert into the mold. Wrap the candy in plastic wrap and tie with an orange ribbon.

■ Make Jell-O Jigglers gelatin snacks. The directions are on the Jell-O box. Cut individual pieces of Jell-O out with pumpkin-shaped cookie cutters. As any parent knows, these treats are a hit at school parties as well as for anytime snacks.

■ Halloween is the children's holiday in our family. One neighbor hung a blanket between the living room and dining room and turned out the lights. A sheet was hung over a coat rack and dim candles lit the room. This mom would hide behind the blanket and eerily groan while the trick-or-treaters came cautiously from behind the curtain to sample witches brew served from a magic caldron — hot chocolate ladled from a big pot.

Costumes. Make a basic costume and change it from year to year. A dalmation this year . . . remove the felt spots, change the ears, add a cotton powder-puff tail and presto . . . the dalmation is transformed to a bunny costume the following year. Use headbands to hold up halos, horns and ears. Use a skirt to fashion a cape.

■ A white bodysuit can be the basic starting point for a Little Mermaid costume by sewing or glueing gold shells on; later it can be used for Snoopy or a polar bear with a few modifications. Just add fur and change the mask and accessories.

■ A simple Superman costume for a little boy is blue underwear, red turtle-neck shirt, a felt "S," a homemade cape and adult knee-highs worn over kid's sneakers (to look like boots).

■ Use makeup rather than masks because you can use it for several years. Makeup is less expensive, too. Look through your makeup case for lipstick, blush, eyeliner and eye shadows. Mix store-bought face makeup with cold cream so it is easy to wash off, or cover your face with cleansing cream before you begin. To make your own face paint mix 1 teaspoon cornstarch and ½ teaspoon cold cream. Blend well. Add ½ teaspoon water. Stir. Add desired color of food coloring and paint design on face with paintbrush or sponge.

■ Search through attics and closets for capes, vests, lace curtains, suspenders, eyeglasses, wigs, ponchos, boots, pocketbooks, scarves, jewelry, hats, sombreros, makeup, Chinese slippers, long red slips . . . all of the components for original costumes. Keep everything in a big box, costume trunk or special bureau, only to be opened right before Halloween.

■ Recycle costumes: Buy or borrow someone else's costume.

Other Holidays

Valentine's Day. On the weekend closest to Valentine's Day, we celebrate "Red Day." The homemade recipe for red play dough is mixed so that each child can make valentine hearts. In addition to the homemade play dough ingredients, containers are filled with scraps of ribbon, crepe paper, glitter and pieces of tin foil. Heart-sticker prizes are awarded to everyone by the parent "judges" who offer lavish praise in the annual awards ceremony for the biggest, smallest, funniest, most original and fanciest valentine heart competition. Each neighbor brings a treat that is red for our snack. Our table is resplendent with strawberry tarts and a sparkling red punch made with red cherries and frozen-juice ice cubes. (Mix one can of red Hawaiian Punch, a six-ounce can of frozen orange juice, a six-ounce can of frozen grape juice, a six-ounce can of frozen lemonade, ginger ale to taste.) Red licorice, red-hot hearts and valentine-shaped taffies color the remainder of the menu.

We begin our festivities by singing "Happy Valentine's Day to You" to the tune of "Happy Birthday" and end with a valentine Heart Hunt. (Hide lots of red construction paper hearts around the room.) Each child dresses up in something red. A tasting contest is always the highlight as the children close their eyes and sample something yummy and red. Strawberry ice cream, a cube of cherry gelatin and red popcorn balls are enjoyed by all.

Thanksgiving. There is much more to Thanksgiving than eating turkey. It is a day to count our blessings and be truly grateful. One family that I know began a tradition of inviting people each year to their home who had nowhere else to go. The children looked forward to sharing their bounty with someone in need, such as a college student who could not afford to go home, an elderly person or a single-parent family. To find people who would love to be the recipients of your generosity, contact churches, adult day-care centers, nursing homes, assisted-living retirement centers, the Coalition for the Homeless, the Pink Ladies (volunteers at hospitals), TLA (To Live Again—a support group for people whose spouses have died), Parents Without Partners and Grandparents' Rights Groups (grandparents who do not see their own grandchildren because of a divorce situation). Or, collect food and donate it to a local church food pantry for needy families.

New Year's. So much fuss is made about New Year's Eve for partying adults. But with the high cost of baby-sitters and the high risk of driving with too many partygoers on the road, try a neighborhood party—kids included. A family volunteers, or is selected by a drawing of straws, for the task of organizing the party. As a group, we come up with decorations, party noisemakers, snacks for the kids and the traditional masks. You celebrate early for the little ones or keep to tradition. Ring bells to welcome in the New Year. Make nonalcoholic champagne—a mixture of club soda, unsweetened fruit juice concentrate, ice cubes and water. Each parent can bring small gifts wrapped with festive-colored paper for the children.

LOW-COST FAMILY VACATION IDEAS

People often say there is no place like home, but there are times that home is the last place you want to be. The following suggestions are low-stress because you will not need a passport, you can skip the fancy wardrobe for those poolside cocktail parties, and you won't have to worry about converting currency . . . since our vacation ideas are of the no-frills variety and affordably priced. You'll find a lot of fun suggestions and money-saving ideas.

Here are some sources of information helpful when planning a vacation:

■ Have the kids help you address postcards requesting information from the state tourist bureaus, chambers of commerce, AAA Motor Clubs, and the travel magazine of the state you would like to visit. You can find this address and telephone information quickly by spending a little time with the reference librarian. As the descriptive brochures arrive, let the kids help you decide what are "must sees."

■ Send a postcard to the Superintendent of Documents, Government Printing Office, Washington, DC 20402 or call (202) 783-3238 and ask for a list of helpful booklets for travelers. There may be a small fee for some booklets and pamphlets to cover the cost of printing and mailing.

■ Investigate guided wilderness trips, pack trips by horse, backpacking, river float trips, canoeing, windjammer cruises, mountaineering, cattle drives, covered wagon treks, cycling, scuba diving trips, trips for teens and other adventures. How do you find such things? Contact various clubs and associations that specialize in conservation or adventurous trips. To name a few organizations: American Forestry Association, National Audubon Society, National Wildlife Federation, Sierra Club and Wilderness Society.

■ Discount travel clubs advertise that they sell unsold seats on airlines and have special block rates on hotel and meal accommodations. You usually pay a membership fee and then you are informed of the specials offered. Check travel magazines and the Sunday newspaper travel section for listings of travel clubs. Check references.

■ Read travel magazines to find information suited to your interests concerning travel tips, places to stay and a variety of vacation information.

■ Visit the library before the trip and check out books about your vacation destination.

Here are some general tips for traveling:

■ Consider traveling off season for better rates and look into vacation spots that are not in the tourist mainstream. A good source of information is a book, *Blue Highways*, that highlights off-the-beaten-track jaunts. The rates will be lower, the tourist traps nonexistent. You can enjoy the privacy of secluded beaches, the sounds of nature and moonlit walks, instead of crowded boardwalks. If you go to a seashore state park, the kids can enjoy playing on the beach, catching crabs and riding on a raft at a well-run facility. Just think, it might not even seem like a vacation because the kids won't be hanging on your leg begging you to buy key chains, coffee mugs, T-shirts and pennants from the overpriced souvenir shops. They may be satisfied with a map you picked up at a gas station or newfound shells or stones from a morning walk on the beach — just make sure the shells are rinsed and checked.

■ Be aware of scams in all travel arrangements such as fraudulent charter flights that have left many tourists stranded at an airport, ticket in hand and no flight in the air. If something appears too good to be true, it probably is. Check the references of all travel groups and clubs. Be sure that former clients have been satisfied with all aspects of the service. Be aware of any limitations and restrictions involved.

■ College students should carry identification cards from their schools for special admittance prices available for students at museums, musical events, hostels and theaters.

■ If a college or church group is sponsoring a charter flight, it is possible that your family can join the group if space is available. The rates on a charter are discounted. We joined a group going to Europe and saved a bundle over the commercial rate.

■ Also consider going on vacation with a family member or friend with whom you are compatible. Splitting vacation expenses on a villa with six bedrooms is a great way to save money. To make multifamily vacations enjoyable for all, give everyone their space, don't overcrowd and select a vacation spot that offers something for everyone.

Do You Have Special Talents?

■ If you are a writer, contact a hotel, airline or resort and suggest writing an article or doing some favorable publicity in exchange for complimentary or reduced-price services or accommodations.

■ Become a "tour director." Contact a travel agent and ask about getting a group together for a trip. If you, as the organizer, get enough people together, make a deal that you and your spouse can go for free. You could gather a group with a particular interest such as church, the environment, a hobby, sport, alumni association or a business organization. Plan a trip that would combine pleasure with a cause or conference.

■ If you have expertise on a topic of general interest and would like to speak on a cruise ship, contact the Director of Entertainment on a cruise line. One friend is doing a tax workshop, another is offering a cooking class, a retired couple is giving bridge lessons and I am doing a talk called "You Ought to Write a Book." In exchange for a few hours of "work" on the ship, my husband and I will get a free cruise vacation to the Caribbean.

Right before you go, remember:

■ Cancel your newspaper service so you are not charged and so burglars are not clued in that you are not home.

■ Don't overpack or you will spend hours arranging and rearranging things to fit everything back into the suitcases, duffle bags and backpacks.

■ Consider taking a helper along, a teenage cousin or friend who can give you a break so you and your spouse can have a "little vacation from the kids."

■ Take your own first-aid kit complete with aspirin, insect repellant, sewing kit, bandages, tweezers and a sunburn soother. I have even taken a small can of disinfectant spray to use on the many germy surfaces you find while on vacation.

Tips for Staying in Hotels

■ Most hotel chains have special pricing for summer or holiday travel. Inquire about family plans and grandparent plans. In some cases, if an adult is over fifty or fifty-five, a special price is in effect. (Be sure the senior has an American Association of Retired Persons [AARP] card, or driver's license to qualify for the special rate.)

■ Clerks often do not tell you about discounted rates when you walk up to a counter; they would prefer you pay the maximum rate, or their rack rate, which is quoted from their standard price list. Contact the central reservation center of the major hotel chains using their 800 number. Inquire about special rates for families and ask for a list of participating hotels. (Some national chains have inns that are privately operated, not corporately owned, so they may not offer the same deals.) There may be some conditions you must meet, such as reservations made in advance, a minimum number of days booked, a limited season, weekend conditions or payment in advance.

■ Local branches of major chains may have additional specials so inquire locally about deals. Always ask for the lowest rate. Ask for specials that include breakfast. Smaller hotels and restaurants may offer a discount for cash because the merchant has to pay approximately 5 percent to the credit card company for the privilege of offering Visa, American Express, MasterCard, etc. If the hotel gives you that discount for cash, you will save a few dollars, there will be no additional paperwork for them, and they still net the same amount for the sale.

The central phone center for hotel reservations and information is listed below. For each of the hotels listed, ask about specials and for the names and locations of participating hotels.

Holiday Inn .... (800) HOLIDAY. Ask about their Great Rates Program.
Sheraton...(800) 325-3535
Marriot (Courtyard) ....(800) 321-2211
Marriot (Residence) ....(800) 331-3131
Days Inn..(800) 325-2525
Super 8 ....(800) 848-8888
Econo Lodges ....(800) 446-6900
Travelodge..(800) 255-3050
Motel 6...(505) 891-6161
Hampton Inns .... (800) HAMPTON
La Quinta ....(800) 531-5900
Red Roof Inns .... (800) THE-ROOF
Embassy Suites...(800) EMBASSY
Guest Quarters ....(800) 424-2900
Radisson Hotels..(800) 333-3333
Quality Suites or Choice Hotel International ....(800) 221-2222
   (This is a central reservation service for seven hotels: Rodeway Inn, Quality Inn, Sleep Inn, Comfort Inn, Clarion, Friendship Inn and Econo Lodges.)

Ask about the following features:

■ Do they offer microwaves, refrigerators, television, telephone, continental breakfast, full breakfast, full kitchen, pool, access to hotel facilities, exercise rooms, coffee and juices in the room in the morning, a happy hour with a free buffet (instead of a dinner)?

■ What is the rate for children? Are children under 18 free?

■ What is the extra person charge?

■ How many people are included in the room fee?

■ Are pets permitted?

■ Is there a late checkout time?

■ Before booking two hotel rooms for your family, inquire about additional cots in one room to accommodate your family.

■ Are rooms guranteed? Until what time?

■ Is a baby-sitting service available?

More hotel tips:

■ Ask if the hotel has any discounts for senior citizens, children, the handi-capped, government employees, students, a trade association with which you are affiliated or military personnel.

■ Do not use phones in the hotel rooms if they charge a service fee for placing the call from your room. Bring your own telephone credit card if you have one. If not, call from a pay phone in the lobby. I recently made ten calls to my husband at home from my hotel. The phone rang and rang, and I was billed by the hotel for all ten "attempted calls" even though I never actually got through.

■ Take your own coffeepot and small packs of tea, coffee and hot chocolate for that first morning cup so you don't have to pay restaurant prices. Save any snacks you did not eat on a flight (and cream, sugar, spoons). Peanuts, peanut butter and jelly, crackers and individually wrapped cheeses come in handy in-stead of room service.

■ Eat at small, local restaurants as opposed to the hotel restaurants.

■ Travel at times when demand for hotel accommodations is low. In other words, don't book a room in Chicago when a major pharmaceutical trade show is going on at the convention hall. Demand is high at that time and so are the rates. It is usually better to stay overnight on the weekends. People in town on com-pany business normally vacate the room for the weekend — most often you can get a discounted rate.

■ Double-check your hotel bill to be sure you have not been overcharged for meals, telephone or bar bills. Suppose someone decided to charge their restau-rant bills to your room. It happened to me while I was watching my pennies — someone else decided to eat and drink heartily and charged everything to my room number. What a surprise at checkout time!

Other places to stay:

■ Bed and breakfasts or "homey" guest houses are available in both city and country settings. You will stay in someone's home, in a spare bedroom, at a cost that is less than most hotels. Depending on the selected facility, you may be served a fancy breakfast by the host family or simple food you might eat at home. You can find guidebooks that list the locations and particulars about bed and breakfasts at the library or bookstore. There is an annual directory by Toni Sortor called *The Annual Directory of American Bed and Breakfasts*. Be sure to inquire if chil-dren are welcome. Not all bed and breakfasts are low cost, so ask for details.

■ Have you ever considered a "Dude Ranch"? A rustic setting, beautiful sce-nery and lots of planned activities await your family with this exciting vacation. Contact the Dude Ranchers Association at (303) 223-8440 for information about ranches in many western states. For about $4, they will send you a thirty-two-page magazine directory listing dude ranch information. Check references before making reservations and sending payment for any vacation spot that is unfamiliar to you.

■ Camping trips are fun for families and an economical way to spend some time communing with nature. There are thousands of public and private campgrounds. Contact the National Park Service for information about national campsites. The library would be a good place to do this type of research. Call scout organizations or travel bureaus in the area you would like to visit. Also, read about camping before you embark on this type of escapade so that it does not become a misadventure. Dig out that old Girl Scout manual for some sage advice. Call an experienced camper and get their advice. There is no sense making your own mistakes if you can learn from the mistakes of others. A voice of experience can give you input about whether to rent, borrow or buy a tent, a camping stove, sleeping bags and cooking equipment. One book I recommend is *Starting Small in the Wilderness: The Sierra Club's Outdoors Guide for Families* by Marilyn Doan. Guidebooks about camping can be found at camping supply stores. Find out about available recreational activities such as swimming, boating, fishing, tennis, nature trails, jogging and bike paths. Most campsites are booked to capacity during the summer months — consider late-spring weekends if reservations weren't made early in the year.

■ Contact travel agents, chambers of commerce and farm organizations to learn about farm resorts where you and the kids can enjoy pigs, ponies, cows and chickens and pick some fruit. The scenery is great and so is the price. My brother let people stay on his farm; he met lots of nice folks who also had a grand time.

■ The American Youth Hostels is a wonderful organization that has comfortable accommodations in the U.S. as well as abroad. I took a bicycle trip one summer and stayed in hostels, which are dormitory-like sleeping arrangements, nothing fancy but the price was right . . . approximately $10 a night. Some sponsor low-cost bike tours in the United States and abroad.

■ Hostels are located in cities in addition to out-of-way countryside locales. When you stay at a hostel, it is fun to take advantage of the touristy and not-so-touristy-type activities in the area. Visit a ranch in Colorado, a lighthouse in California, the forest recreational areas in Oregon, or ride the swan boats in Boston's Public Garden. To find out more about hostels write to American Youth Hostels Association, Box 37613, Washington, DC 20013-7613, (202) 783-6161. They can also provide information about the International Youth Hostel Federation.

■ Many college dormitories are not used during the summer. Inquire about your family staying in a dorm room for a few nights while you take in the sights of the area of your choice. There is a book called *Let's Go* that gives information about this type of accommodation. I did this when I attended a library trade show in California. After the airline expense incurred traveling from one coast to the other, I wanted to save where I could. The dorm charge was $10 per night. The hotel would have been $85. I used the school's facilities, such as the tennis court, pool and library — a real bargain for $10 — and I even enjoyed the cafeteria food and the college atmosphere.

■ Switch houses with a friend or acquaintance in a distant city. We invited someone from Tennessee to stay in our house and we stayed in theirs. After agreeing on the dates, we made the switch. They loved our house and we loved theirs. Besides cutting down on the expense of lodging, by cooking your meals in their kitchen you can eliminate expensive restaurant meals. We made a list of the highlights they should visit in our area, and they left maps and guidebooks for us.

■ My brother and his wife took this idea one step further and traded homes with a family in Heidelburg, Germany. They took in the castles and enjoyed the wonderful cuisine of Europe while the other family enjoyed staying on their farm in Pennsylvania.

■ There is an organization called Vacation Exchange Club. For a free information pack, write P.O. Box 820, Haleiwa, HI 96712 or call (800) 638-3841 or Intervac U.S. and International Home Exchange, P.O. Box 590504, San Francisco, CA 94159, (415) 435-3497.

■ Offer to "house-sit" for someone who is going to be away, preferably in a resort or affluent area. Water their plants, feed their pets, read their local newspaper and attend local events, use their pool, have a change of scenery and be paid, too! Put a notice on the community bulletin board, advertise in a classified ad, register with a bonded house-sitting service and let others know you are available. (My brother and his wife do this for people who live along the Philadelphia Main Line. The homes are in the million-dollar plus range, so this is truly a vacation idea.)

General Transportation Tips

■ Over and over again, I hear experienced travelers say to book early for airfares and ask for the best rate for hotel accommodations. There are often twelve different airfares that can be billed for a flight. If you are flexible about travel times and routes (which may not be direct and have layovers), you can save significantly. Ask about the "red eye" flights where you fly late at night and arrive at your destination in the middle of the night or early morning. Ask the price if you fly "standby" or if you stay over a Saturday night. After you are quoted a rate, ask if there's a better rate.

■ Insist on the best rate. This has worked on many occasions for me. They profit by renting the room, and the restaurant and souvenir shop may benefit from your cash.

■ Make good friends with a travel agent. The ideal choice of an agent is someone who has been referred to you by a friend or relative. A competent travel agent knows about the best deals, the latest rates and best ways to travel. Be aware that they get paid on commission. Since they want your business in the future as well as now, they usually have your best interest at heart.

■ Read *The Airline Passenger's Guerrilla Handbook*, by George Albert Brown, for strategies to beat the air travel system. Distributed by Slawson Communications, Inc. (800) SLAWSON.

■ My parents take Amtrak to Florida. When traveling via train, ask about special train fares for adults and children traveling together. Ask about any unusual vacations coast-to-coast or within a region. Inquire about senior citizen rates. Travel discounts may be limited to certain times. Call (800) USA-RAIL for Amtrak train and fare information.

■ How about a Greyhound or Continental Trailways bus vacation? There are passes available for unlimited travel for one price within a certain period of time and geographic area.

■ A friend who works for an airline advised me to book early because most of the economical rates for fares apply only to a limited number of seats. The first-come, first-served maxim applies here if you want to save money on airline tickets. Ask about supersavers, off-peak travel time and excursion fares. Be aware that many of the specials come with no-refund policies and you may not be able to change flight plans by time or date.

■ Airlines often overbook but will offer compensation to passengers who give up their seat, foregoing the overcrowded flight to accept another. If you don't mind the inconvenience and the delay in your travel plans, you might appreciate the money saved or even a free ticket.

■ If you have to travel for a funeral, contact the airlines. Most offer a special rate for emergencies that have to be booked without advance notice.

General Tips for Traveling With Kids

■ Involve everyone in the planning stages of the trip. "Who wants to sightsee? Who wants to visit our cousins? Who wants to just go to a beach and lay out in the sun? Each family member has a different idea for the makings of a good vacation. Of course, in the end, you try to accommodate everyone.

■ Take favorite blankets and stuffed animals, a familiar music box to lull a child to sleep and extra baby bottles for infants and toddlers (our trip to Des Moines was ruined by forgetting these essentials — the result was an inconsolable two-year-old for most of the night and extremely tired parents the next day).

■ Avoid taking toys that have small pieces, horns, dolls that talk repetitively, whistles, and toys with sticks that could poke and injure.

■ Have a pack prepared with books, snacks, stickers, small games, coloring books, flash cards, markers, crayons, magnetic games and doodle paper to keep kids happy in the car, plane, train, restaurant or hotel room.

■ Pack brown-bag surprises and pull them out when you feel you are going to pull your hair out because of the whining, pinching, poking or loud laughing (or was that crying?). Keep little juice packs, favorite snacks, fruit snacks and granola treats ready for those "just in case all else fails" occasions. Word-search and puzzles games, tic-tac-toe, a deck of playing cards and paper dolls can keep kids occupied when other things have failed.

■ Carry lots of moist towelettes. You will need them a million times during a vacation . . . trust me.

■ Have coloring books and crayons to occupy kids in restaurants while waiting for food. Ask the waitress for saltines while waiting for the meals to be cooked.

■ Buy a map and let the kids mark important landmarks and things they have enjoyed about the trip on the map.

■ Bring a keepsake notebook to use as a journal and to glue postcards, brochures and souvenir memorabilia from the trip.

■ You must childproof your hotel room as carefully as your home. A crib near a hotel window without a screen or outlet covers that have not been plugged with protective caps are just as dangerous in the hotel as at home.

■ Bring story and song cassettes. Bring a radio with headphones for the teenager who does not care to listen to nursery rhymes and fairy tales suited for younger children.

■ Rotate seats, including mom and dad, for a change of scenery and conversation.

■ Stop frequently to stretch if on a car trip. Play ball, run around and do what you have to so the kids are not cooped up too long.

■ Consider staying in hotels that are not in the middle of the city. Playgrounds are a great tourist attraction for kids. If your hotel is in the suburbs near a playground, the kids can get some exercise before you embark on the day's travels.

■ Schedule rest stops at the fast-food restaurants that have play areas.

Play car games such as:

1. Counting license plates from each state — list all the states or use a map, put a check when you spot a car from that state.

2. Scavenger hunt — prior to the trip, write a list of things you want to spot and allocate points for a brick building, a horse, a green and yellow sign, Burger King, a lady with an umbrella, etc.

3. Play the alphabet game — start with "A," and everyone looks for something that begins with "A." The first person to spot an "apple stand" gets a point. Next

try to find something that begins with "B." If someone spies a boat on a trailer, then a point is given. Continue until the end of the alphabet or interest wanes.

4a. Think of all the girls' names that begin with a certain letter, for example "K" — Kathy, Katelyn, Kelly, etc.

4b. Name all of the things associated with Christmas — for example, ornament, gingerbread house, Santa Claus, greeting cards.

4c. Think of all the things that can fly — for example, helicopter, insect, kite, helium balloon.

5. Count the cows game — count the cows on each side of the road, but if you pass a school on your side of the car, you "lose" all of your cows (or whatever you decide to count). Set a goal, such as whoever has the most cows (points) by the time we get to Belvedere or the first one to get thirty cows wins.

6. Pick a place that you are hiding — one person pretends to be hiding and gives clues — the others ask questions such as "Are you on earth?" "Are you higher or lower than this car?"

These ideas that have worked for my family and friends were put together in a conscious attempt to increase the excitement of summer and weekends with a special interest toward developing lasting friendships and strengthening family ties.

Happy trails to you!

CHAPTER SIX

Kids' Rooms and Stuff

A child's room is a special place and often means more than just a comfortable, safe place to sleep. My children like to think of it as their secret place or a "house within a house," and they take pride in using every nook and cranny to design their personal space. Their alcoves are sometimes places to share the secrets of school life with friends and sometimes private, relaxing worlds of imaginative play providing many hours of fun.

The nursery will all too soon become the homework area of a school-age child or teenager. It is advisable to anticipate the interests of the future. As children grow, their tastes change and colorful circus themes are replaced by more sophisticated schemes. You don't want to be caught off guard when you do not have a big budget to update a room to a more dignified style.

When decorating and organizing a room, it is best to think not only of the needs of the kids but yours as well. Most parents do not favor a room that is filled with chaos. "A place for everything and everything in its place" seems to be the tape that plays in the minds of most parents. The ideas that follow will give you solutions for keeping even the most unorganized kids organized with a room that could be shown to unexpected company. Lots of imaginative ways to hide cumbersome clutter, tidy up the closet, manage the clothes and put to good use wall and floor space will be explored.

You will also see that by accessorizing with a variety of baskets, kites, wind socks, colorful bed linens, wall hangings, glue-on graphics and flea market finds, you can give a new dimension to a child's room.

Don't forget that your library is a great resource for how-to and do-it-yourself books and videos for enterprising homeowners. There are many sources of information that address home decorating, building and finishing techniques, landscape design, picture framing and wall displays.

Look into local noncredit classes like wallpapering, refinishing and stenciling. Craft stores and wallpaper stores also offer classes at a nominal fee or no cost because the merchants expect to get your business when you buy supplies.

GENERAL TIPS FOR DECORATING A CHILD'S ROOM

Some children have specific ideas about how they would like their rooms decorated. Their idea of a child's delight may not be your vision at all. Your flowered-print bedspread pales in comparison to the Little Mermaid one they saw in a friend's bedroom. Their personalities, ages and tastes will affect what they want in the room you plan to "facelift." *Warning:* Before you go to great trouble and expense designing a Wizard of Oz, space shuttle or dinosaur motif, encourage your child to participate in the planning phase. Do a little window shopping together looking at fabric swatches, paint-sample charts, wallpaper books, designs and color schemes. Better to hear the word "yuck" before you spend countless hours of labor and your hard-earned cash rather than after.

When preparing the nursery for a new baby, think ahead a year or two. Try to decorate so that the look can be updated as the child grows older. Keep in mind that you won't want to totally redecorate from the Mother Goose to the Ninja-Turtle stage. As the child outgrows the baby decor, it is desirable to add a few items that reflect new interests rather than to begin anew.

One of the quickest ways to add new life to a drab room is a fresh coat of paint, which is available in an infinite number of exciting colors. Paint in a light shade to make a room appear larger. Try a different color of paint to accent door frames, window trim and moldings. Even though painting seems like a relatively easy job, requiring no special skills other than a steady hand, check out a book from the library and do a little homework before tackling this job. A few pages of reading can help you avoid some painting pitfalls, like failing to prepare wall surfaces properly, purchasing cheap paint or using the wrong type. Pointers on when to use latex or enamel, how to apply paint for a smooth look, how to mix paint and other tricks of the trade can be found by reading a how-to book or taking a free seminar on painting offered at many home-center decorating stores.

■ Jazz up a dull area with some glow-in-the-dark paint. (How about stars painted on the ceiling or rocket ships blasting off?) If a child is afraid of the dark, perhaps some brightness will help.

■ We had a friend who drew animal cartoonlike characters and turned a bedroom wall into a menagerie of adorable animals a la Disney-like characters. For an older child, paint a zoo scene with a natural-looking habitat of trees, grass, water, open skies complete with river otters, lions, snow leopards and other frisky critters.

■ Reproduce the pattern of the bedspread as a design on a wall. If the bedspread is a pink-and-white floral design, paint a pink-and-white floral design on the wall as a border or as a focal point.

■ Another way to redecorate a room is to paint it and add a decorative border. To minimize the cost of a border, buy a wide section and cut it in half lengthwise. Now you have twice as much length, just thinner. For example, if the border has four blue-and-white stripes, you will have a border of two stripes for trimming the room. This "thin border" can be used to decorate around the windows and door of a room too!

■ If you don't want to wallpaper a whole room, paint and then add colorful touches. Buy a few rolls of "race car" wallpaper, and wallpaper the lightswitch, outlet covers and the heating vents in a young boy's room. (Cover the vents with paper and then cut the slits for the air to come through.) Or cover a jewelry box, hamper and wastebasket. Cut out a few pieces and decorate the walls in the closet.

■ Inexpensive odd rolls of colorful wallpaper purchased at garage sales are great as shelf paper in a kid's closet.

■ A money-saving tip is to always check the "cut-up" bin in a home center. This pile will have lots of interesting odds and ends such as colorful molding, plywood, pieces of Formica, and decorative accents.

Furniture

Ask around if you are in the market for kids' furniture. My sister-in-law had her heart set on a white-and-gold French Provincial furniture set for her daughter's bedroom. The department store prices were out of her range. I knew someone who wanted to sell — the sale was made and everyone was happy!

Buy floor-model furniture at a discount and go to "unsold freight" warehouses for bargain furniture.

Did you know that you can wallpaper old cabinets, or badly nicked bookcases, giving new life to surfaces other than walls? Check at the wallcovering store for odd lots of wallpaper that will match your decorating scheme. You will find attractive designs that are heavily discounted by stores trying to get rid of leftover odds and ends. Ask about the procedures for using wallpaper on a surface other than walls.

Wooden trunks can be decoupaged, spray painted or stenciled. For design ideas, check greeting-card borders, wallpaper books, and the designs on a bedspread, curtain or sheet for simple-to-duplicate ideas. Stencil a child's name, the ABC's, numbers or a phrase or two from a poem or nursery rhyme. Buy patterned self-stick adhesive floor tiles and "tile" the top and sides. Consider a new finish for an old trunk by covering it with wallpaper that coordinates with the paint on the walls or the pattern of the bedspread.

If you do not have small children and have a trunk that can be left open without the threat of injury, you might consider decorating the trunk both inside and out. A friend cuts sheets, curtains and wallpaper pieces to size. She suggests "painting on glue" one section at a time for the interior and covering the surface of the inside of the trunk, section by section. She has even stapled sheets and curtain material to the outside of the trunk for a very fitted look. Don't worry about trimming off the edges inside or out because you can cover with ribbon, rick-rack or braided cord along any unfinished edges.

After giving furniture a fresh coat of paint, stencil or sponge-paint a design. (You can also sponge-paint and stencil lampshades.)

Tips for Sponge Painting: Cut the desired shape from a clean sponge, for example, a heart shape. Dip in paint and squeeze out very well so that it is almost dry. Sponges are very absorbent but you want an almost dry sponge. Dab on a paper towel or newspaper so most of the paint is removed and there is no excess dripping. You do not want a "blob" effect. Imprint your design on the desired surface. Try sponge-painting on lampshades, lamp bases (not the shiny ceramic type), trunks, pottery, walls and even on the little stepladders that help small children reach the sink.

Some quick tips for furniture fix-ups:

■ A home-supply store usually has a variety of ways to add letters of a child's name to his or her room. Adhesive-backed letters of the mailbox variety, or plastic or wooden letters to spray-paint can be the beginning of a personal touch. Place the letters on the door, or on a wall, bureau or shelf. Stencil with cutouts of lettering on the outside of the door.

■ Many libraries have books with stencil design patterns that you can check out. Add some flowers, animals and stars to the door. Make a print of your child's hand and put it on the door. (You can always paint over it as tastes change!)

■ You can applique cutouts to decorate window shades in a room. Use a favorite theme such as cars, flowers, animals, ballerinas, cartoon characters or space figures. Get wallpaper or upholstery fabric books from stores that are tossing them out. Cut out the decorations and glue them to the shade. Be careful to evaluate your design and type of shade (fabric, cotton or vinyl) so that it does not "crinkle" when you roll up the shade.

■ Let your child personalize a plain lampshade by gluing pictures of interesting things from magazines and catalogs. Add decorative touches such as figures that are cut from those outdated wallpaper books you obtained at no charge from a store. Cutouts of animal figures, nursery-rhyme characters or the pattern that matches your wallpaper is a secondary use of leftover wallpaper.

■ Poke pinholes in a plain shade to allow light to shine through. For example, poke holes in the shape of a flower or a bear for an interesting effect when the light is turned on.

Fun With Fabrics

■ Bedspreads and quilts are expensive items if purchased at department stores. Instead, buy material at a fabric store and make your own bedspread by just hemming the edges of the material. (One clever mom sewed a few end-of-season priced beachtowels together to make an inexpensive bedspread for a twin bed.)

■ With a little extra material and effort, you can make matching curtains. For a shortcut on both time and money, make window swags or valances, which require very little material. There are even special hooks that make it easy to drape fabric for a fashionable curtain look with no sewing required. Check the remnant tables at a fabric store or flea market for inexpensive lace or fringe to add your own custom touches.

■ Ask your local wallpaper and paint stores for their discontinued wallpaper books that contain samples as well as swatches of material. You can sew the sample swatches together for a quilted-look bedspread and curtains. Once again, consider cutting out a picture or pattern from the wallpaper pages and gluing to wastebaskets, hampers and lampshades.

■ Fabric paint (make sure it's the kind that won't come off in the washer), available at arts-and-crafts and fabric stores, is a simple method for converting plain sheets (bought on sale) into designer-looking curtains, bedspread, pillowcases and wall hangings. Decide on the pattern you want and use the fabric paints to create a special effect that won't wash off. We used a product called "Liquid Embroidery" that didn't fade or wash off.

■ To make simple inexpensive cafe curtains, buy an extra pillowcase to match your bed linens. Cut open along the seam one side of the pillowcase and continue cutting along the bottom seam. Open the pillowcase so that it is now one large piece. Insert a curtain rod through the wide hem opening. You now have cafe curtains to match the bedsheets.

■ Curtains can also be made from a flat twin sheet. There is a two-inch hem at the top of the sheet. Insert a curtain rod through the already-opened hem. Use pretty ribbon or braided cord for tiebacks.

■ Buy an interesting piece of material that coordinates with the bedspread or curtain and stretch the material over a wooden frame. Staple the edges of the material to the back of the frame for a great wall hanging.

■ Select a print or pattern that goes with your bedspread or curtains and make a bureau scarf, doily, throw pillow or pillowcase. Check with the personnel of a fabric or craft store for new sewing and nonsewing innovations. Glue guns and fabric glue may mean that you don't even have to sew in the traditional sense to make these things.

■ Make decorative throw pillows for the bed. Simple animal faces and colorful geometric patterns are always popular. This is one project that fabric glue makes especially quick and easy. Buy a pillow form. Buy fabric and cut squares or desired shape one inch larger all around than the pillow form. Sew or glue the edges of the fabric on all but one side. Put the pillow form in. Sew or glue the last side. Attach felt shapes for eyes and nose or simply make designs. If you plan to wash the pillow frequently, it would be best to sew the designs on. If the pillow is just a decorative touch for the room, use fabric glue.

■ A fun-looking, easy-to-make pillow can be crafted with a pillowcase, a long tube-shaped pillow form, and two lengths of ribbon. Put the pillow form inside the pillowcase. Twist each end of the pillowcase and tie up the ends with ribbon.

(Picture how a piece of pink bubblegum or saltwater taffy is wrapped.) Now you have a decorative pillow that matches your bed linens.

■ To jazz up plain sheets and pillowcases, cut out colorful figures of sailboats, teddy bears, balls, rag dolls or balloons from festive prints or patterned fabrics. Colorful material from a remnant, old curtain or pillowcase also works. Cut figures out of a brown paper bag first to use as a pattern for your character or simple design. Use the pattern to trace the figure on the material, cut out and then sew your design onto the edges of the sheets and pillowcases for a custom look. Don't sew or glue the "applique" onto any part that a child will sleep on because it would be uncomfortable.

■ For plain sheets and pillowcases, sew lace around the edges of the pillowcase and onto the part of the top sheet that folds down.

■ When a bedspread or quilt becomes stained with the dog's footprints or torn by energetic kids jumping on the bed, it can sometimes be salvaged. Quilts are expensive and worth repairing. When my son's became stained with red juice, I cut out a design from a coordinating piece of material and appliqued the design over the damaged section — or buy fabric glue and glue it on in two minutes! I added a few rocking horse designs to the bold blue-and-white striped bedspread. For a small tear, embroider something cute to cover the hole.

■ When you tire of the tiebacks on the kid's curtains or, more likely, one tieback has mysteriously disappeared (and you later find it in the basement where it has been creatively recycled by your six-year-old as a leash for a stuffed animal that needed a walk), buy some brightly colored ribbon, rosettes, fringe or remnant material in a coordinating pattern and make a new pair of tiebacks to update and beautify the window treatment.

Creative Wall Hangings

■ Buy a large map to use as a low-cost and educational wall decoration. A large chalkboard on the wall is also a nifty idea. You can buy a product called chalkboard paint at local paint stores. Applying this paint to any hard surface, such as a wall, closet door or the side of a bureau, converts just about anything to a chalkboard. Cut a sheet of Masonite to a design that suits you and apply the chalkboard paint for a truly customized conversation piece. Add a box of colored chalk and you have an instant easel that exhibits your young artist's talent and current interests. Or simply attach a mural-size sheet of clear plastic to the wall and provide washable markers for the artist in the room.

■ To make a bulletin board, buy corkboard and mount it on the door. Adhesive-backed carpet squares can also be arranged to make a bulletin board. Keep a supply of colored straight pins or tacks handy to display those starred test papers.

■ Buy several brightly colored cloth kites or cotton wind socks that are available in a variety of designs. Basic two-dollar kites are also fine but the fabric types, such as those in the shape of interesting sea creatures, make enchanting wall and ceiling decorations. Mount them on the wall or ceiling for a colorful decorating touch that floats across the room.

■ Make a wall hanging using a variety of colorful felt swatches. Buy felt by the yard or pieces of remnant felt. Cut out shapes of multicolored felt to glue onto the main background piece. If you do not have faith in your ability to draw, trace a stencil on a piece of felt with chalk and cut out the stencil design. Use hot glue or tacky glue to attach the small felt to the main piece. Some people even layer the pieces of felt for an interesting effect. Sew or glue a hem along the top of the main piece of felt. Slide a wooden dowel through the hem. Use string or yarn to hang it on the wall.

■ Assemble a jigsaw puzzle on a piece of cardboard large enough to hold the completed puzzle. When the puzzle is complete, place another piece of cardboard on top of it. Flip it over carefully so the blank side of the puzzle is facing up. Apply rubber cement to make the puzzle adhere to the cardboard. Mount on the wall when completely dry.

■ Go through your box of extra photographs, the ones that never made it to frames or albums. Cut out the faces of kids, little babies, puppies, birthday parties, parents, grandparents, etc., and make a collage. Size the pictures and glue onto a piece of cardboard. Put the family history in an inexpensive Plexiglas frame and mount it on the wall. Or simply put on heavy cardboard and make a frame using colored tape or strips of pretty wrapping paper or wallpaper as a border. Great to give as gifts to family members, too!

■ Adapt the above idea to make a collage of pictures of favorite things cut out from magazines and greeting cards. Or souvenirs from a vacation such as ticket stubs, postcards and snapshots. Glue the treasures to an old window shade, note the year or grade of the child on the reverse side. Roll up the old shade for posterity and roll out a new one each year. Shades are a handy way to display items and easy to store too.

■ Take a favorite photograph to a copy center and have it enlarged to poster size in black and white or color. Frame it and hang it on a door or wall. Very inexpensive and delightful, a neat way to personalize any room.

■ Frame a special greeting card in an inexpensive frame. If a storybook is damaged, consider removing the cover or a few favorite illustrations and framing them in dime-store frames. Keep your eye out for frames at flea markets. A little spray paint can make them as good as new in seconds.

KEEPING KIDS ORGANIZED

Sometimes a bedroom should be divided to make two smaller rooms in the interest of peace, independence and privacy. One sibling may have to get up early for the 7:12 school bus, and you definitely don't need a toddler awake that early. The solution is to partition the room so that each person has her own refuge. You could install a modular unit yourself or hire someone to construct a dividing wall. Folding screens or floor-to-ceiling dividers are an inexpensive way to partition a room. Folded doors suspended from the ceiling or an arrangement of attractive bookshelves or furniture can give the appearance of separate areas for multiage children crowded into close quarters. Always consider "safety first" when building or installing cabinets, bookcases and shelves. Kids have a primal instinct to climb, and any structure that is not secure could be dangerous if it falls on a child. Properly mount, firmly attach and assemble such units according to directions and good judgment.

Don't forget the value of bunk beds for siblings crowded into a small room. Saving space by sleeping one child above another frees up space for a play area, cabinets, bookcase, desk, bureau and shelves. When you need to conserve space, bunk beds are a necessity.

Keeping organized in the bedroom can be a real challenge. Since my kids seem to have inherited a "pack rat gene" from me, it is handy to place like things in a particular bin. Try to keep rooms uncluttered! Store things neatly in boxes under the bed so that primarily they are out of sight and maybe even organized. (Let's not push it. One out of two isn't bad.)

Below are some ideas for storage receptacles:

■ Use plastic milk crates to design a child-friendly but neat environment. They are now sold as storage boxes in variety stores.

■ Buy plastic buckets for storage of toys.

■ Hardware and sporting goods stores sell bait boxes and plastic tool boxes that compartmentalize miniature toys very nicely.

■ Save a variety of boxes and containers — all shapes and sizes. Cigar boxes, shoe boxes, potato chip cylinders, coffee cans, egg cartons, gift boxes, hat boxes, etc. Cover them with attractive wallpaper or adhesive-backed shelf paper and use for bureau catchalls. Decorate with various trimmings from the fabric store.

■ Multicolored crates are great for storing toys. Blocks go in one and stuffed animals in the other. By separating crayons, art supplies, Legos and blocks, you will find that pieces stay intact and the room has a semblance of organization. In our house, one bin is allocated for each of the following: books, socks, puppets, art supplies and stuffed animals.

■ Use wooden fruit crates for storage. The compartmentalized ones for oranges can be painted in joyful colors and hung on the wall to store little collectibles.

■ Even old drawers from a bureau you are about to discard (or someone else has at their curb) can be saved and given a second chance. Paint the drawers in a bright colors and use them as closet storage bins or hideaway bins for under the bed.

- Hang a shoebag as a catchall for diapers, pins, powder, lotion, etc.

- Save decorative baby-print gift bags (such as the ones you find in the Hallmark stores) to keep powder, cotton balls, lotion and pins organized neatly in place on the dresser. Also save those decorative kiddie gift bags to store videogames neatly on a bureau.

- Yard sales or thrift shops are great places to pick up large trunks and chests that can double as conversation pieces and storage receptacles. Store items such as greeting cards, baby clothes and family sentimental objects.

- Trunks are also great for storing coats out of season. Be sure you can lock the trunk securely. Lids on trunks can be very heavy. Children have been seriously injured when a lid closed as they were reaching in. (I would not use anything with a lid as a toy box for small children — even lightweight ones are painful on small fingers. However, trunks are wonderful for other applications, just remember the natural curiosity of children and use them wisely.)

- An old hamper can be updated with a new look and a new purpose. Paint in bright colors and place one in each child's room. Use the hamper as a hideaway area to store out-of-season clothes folded neatly out of sight.

- One mother puts a colorful laundry basket with handles in each room. Each child is responsible for carrying their soiled clothes to the laundry room on Monday and from the laundry room on Tuesday.

- Make a simple, portable toy box by bolting caster wheels to the bottom of a wooden box or fruit crate. This toys-on-wheels contraption can roll around from room to room. It can be quickly hidden in a closet at cleanup time. Avoid any wooden boxes with sharp wires.

- Large cylindrical barrels used by moving companies can be painted and decorated with wallpaper or adhesive-backed paper to serve as a hamper or out-of-season clothes storage bin. If there is any danger of your child climbing or falling in and being hurt, save this for when the child is school-age.

- Save barrels when you move or call a mover in the Yellow Pages and ask if they have any slightly damaged barrels. They also are available in a small size. I have seen a "half barrel" spray-painted and stenciled with an alphabet and number design that was used for toys in a child's room.

- Try a screw and nail organizer that has several little drawers or a shoebag with lots of compartments for art supplies.

- Baskets are great as catchalls for storing miscellaneous treasures and perceived heirlooms, toys, crayons, dress-up clothes and other collectible debris. If they are wicker baskets, they can be painted or stenciled.

- Plastic stacking shoe boxes are great storage bins. Permanent markers used to label the contents of plastic bins work fine. For a younger child, glue a cut-out picture that shows what goes in the bin to the front of the bin. For example, crayons go in a bin with a picture of a box of crayons and the word "crayons" on the front. This is also a wonderful learning tool for teaching reading fundamentals to preschoolers.

■ Low shelves can be made by placing a piece of Plexiglas or wood across cinder blocks. Trucks, dolls and favorite games are conveniently displayed at a child's level. Crates are great for storing books. Shop the flea markets for old mailboxes or breadboxes. Enhance with Contact paper, paint or add a few decals and you have another place to store (hide) things.

■ A second clothing rod placed beneath the primary rod will give you twice as much room to hang clothes in the closet. Adults can reach the clothes on the upper pole while young ones learn to independently care for clothes at their level. Even a three-year-old who cannot reach hangers on a normal-height rod can learn to hang up a jacket if the rod is low. Install low-hanging hooks in the children's closet on the back wall. They'll have no excuse to say they can't put away their own outfits — make that one less excuse!

■ As you collect paper-bag puppets, greeting cards, tickets to Walt Disney World and such memorabilia, meant to be kept forever, save them in a special-memories box hidden on the top shelf of your closet. But for those millions of other not-so-important scraps that are special to your youngster, buy a length of ribbon, two or three inches wide, and attach the important items with stick pins, one under the other. Pin artwork, postcards, gold-starred test papers and souvenirs, hanging vertically. Attach the top of the ribbon to the wall (picture how people display their Christmas cards pinned one beneath the other on a pretty piece of grosgrain ribbon).

LOW-COST PLAYTHINGS

I remember all of the wonderful times I had as a kid when we transformed simple, everyday household items with a healthy dose of energy and imagination into an endless variety of playthings. The following ideas listed are for inexpensive things that will provide hours of enjoyment for children. If you do decide to purchase toys, buy toys that will serve multiage groups and abilities. A sturdy set of blocks can be enjoyed by preschoolers and elementary age. The same principle applies for Legos and most construction-type toys. Don't buy toys based on price alone. It is better to purchase high-quality toys that will last beyond Christmas morning. It is inconvenient to have to return or replace toys, especially since the box is usually the first casualty — most never survive the opening.

Creative Playthings products may at first glance seem expensive but they've survived our playroom for eight years. The items in the Environments catalog are also highly recommended. Call (800) EI-CHILD for a free catalog. Also, in my opinion, Little Tikes playthings are priced right and prove durable. And if you are buying toys or sport equipment in a retail store, don't hesitate to ask the manager for a markdown if the items are scratched, found to have missing pieces, or seem defective. Fix the problem yourself and take advantage of a discount. Buy toys in discount stores whenever possible. They can be half the price of a regular toy store.

Scissors, paper, glue, clay and crayons allow a child to express feelings through art. Kids like to get involved in projects, especially if there are no right or wrong ways to construct and create. Simple art materials are available at reasonable prices. Ask your newspaper publisher to save "end rolls" for you. These large rolls of white paper are perfect for hours of delightful play by future Rembrandts.

Here are some ideas for playtime that won't cost much:

■ A kid's playhouse can be as complex or simple as you desire. With hammer and nails, you can construct a clubhouse from leftover pieces of wood. If you have a suitable tree, consider making a tree house and teaching the kids how to climb safely. If carpentry isn't your thing, simply clear out a closet and let the kids pile up blankets, pillows and an old rug or two. Or cover a cardtable with a blanket. Their imagination will take it from there.

■ Adding inexpensive curtain-type material around the top bunk bed transforms a sleeping area into a new playhouse. The bottom bunk is now a cozy home or a hideaway area.

■ Cardboard boxes painted and taped together provide hours of creative fun. You might want to supervise the cutting out of doors and windows. My children draw pictures that they hang in the "elegant interior" of their cardboard-box home. Given a few props, such as an old rug and a flashlight, they are thrilled to have their own clubhouse. (Ask appliance stores if you can have their large cardboard-box discards.)

■ Camping out inside is a fun experience for youngsters. Set up a pup tent for a perfect indoor-camping experience. Set it up in your living room and tuck your children into their sleeping bags or on foam or air mattresses. For this special night, they can stay awake as long as they want and have a "campfire" snack such as marshmallows. Insist it be truly primitive — with no fire!

■ A magnifying glass is an inexpensive plaything that can provide interesting challenges and new lessons. Looking at ordinary objects, such as twigs, insects, beads of water, grass or pavement through a plastic magnifying glass is fun for children of all ages.

■ Save all kinds of squirt bottles for water-play fun: lemon juice-type, dish detergent. . . .

■ Remember Candy Land, Monopoly, Parcheesi and Twister? Make your own supersize versions of popular games by using large blank sheets of newsroll or cardboard boxes to replicate the original game board. Instead of using the colored plastic markers, walk through the moves yourself. This can also be the low-cost theme for a great children's party. If you have an uncarpeted floor area, consider using special, removable tape to outline a game design, such as hopscotch or tic-tac-toe. You can buy colored masking tape. Use blazing primary colors to add pizzazz.

■ When you lose the pieces to a favorite game or someone has used the money from Monopoly to play "store" in the basement, it is time to recycle the game and use your imagination to make up new rules with the old board and remaining pieces. Combine the pieces from several "orphaned" games to create new ones.

■ Don't forget the basics of board games: games like Scrabble, Concentration, Cootie, Dominoes, Checkers and Boggle have provided fun for all ages for many years. With just a deck of cards, a lifelong pastime of relaxing with card games can begin. Fish, War, Old Maid, Rummy, Snap, Hearts and Crazy Eights are easy to learn.

■ Used truck tires are easy to obtain at truck service stations or supply shops. Usually yours for the asking, these large tractor or truck tires have multiple entertainment possibilities for kids. A large tire can be converted into a swing or backyard climbing toy. With rope, screws, imagination and some elbow grease to wash away the grime, you can construct swings, climbing poles and a variety of playthings. Check the local playgrounds and see how they have constructed the play equipment made from tires and tubes. Safety first is the primary consideration, so be sure everything is bolted properly. Another use for a large tire is to make a sandbox. Fill one with 50 pounds of sand purchased at a garden center, hardware store or lumberyard. Poke holes on the interior rim of the tire so rainwater drains out, thus no worms stay in.

■ Use milk cartons for building blocks. Open the peak of the milk carton. Wash thoroughly and allow to dry. Tape the tops shut and cover with adhesive-backed paper. Save boxes in a variety of shapes and sizes. Add these to your traditional block collection. Boxes of all sizes can be used to make a miniature city, a castle or igloo. Giant boxes can be adorned using crayons or markers or decorated with fabric and wallpaper.

■ On the reverse side of a plastic tablecloth, shirt cardboard or shower curtain, draw a series of roads, houses, farms, trees and so on. Keep a box of plastic animals, pipe cleaners and small cars handy. You'll find the children can amuse themselves for quite a while with this activity. They will make pretend towns and pipe cleaner people. Make the play area a map of your local community and have them find the way to the grocery store, the library and their school.

To begin a collection of useful items to make inexpensive toys and games, ask the following merchants or plant supervisors to save their "about-to-be-discarded" items for you.

The following is a list of locations where I have obtained free arts-and-crafts supplies:

Paint store—sample paint charts

Lumberyard — scraps of wood
Carpet store — floor samples
Fabric store — spools, scraps, eyelet, ribbon
Tobacco shop — cigar boxes
Printer — all sizes, shapes and textures of paper
Garment factory — pieces of fabric
Label factory — stickers
Moving companies and furniture stores — large boxes
Computer Centers — printout paper

Start an arts-and-crafts supply arsenal for rainy day and "I'm so bored" days. Include: margarine containers, plastic lids of all sizes, empty oatmeal containers, old magazines and catalogs, baby-food jars, egg cartons, heavy string, half-gallon milk containers, paper plates, old calendars, wrapping paper scraps, old greeting cards, pinecones, foil, junk mail, frozen juice cans, ribbon and yarn. You are sure to think of many more.

SURVIVING THE "EVERYONE IN MY CLASS HAS ONE" SYNDROME

As adults, we know that sometimes there just isn't money for what we want; sometimes there isn't even money for what we need. Kids don't always understand that.

It just isn't possible to keep up with the Joneses and it isn't healthy to try either. Even though you don't want your kids to feel out of place or inferior because they are wearing the no-frills brand sneakers, it isn't within most budgets to buy the best of everything.

Several friends are experiencing the frustration of having teenagers who are adamant about what they will and will not wear. Adolescents are not usually enthralled by the idea of wearing someone else's hand-me-downs. When your family austerity plan is in effect, creativity is the key to a well-dressed child and peace in the household.

Communication is critical, too. Your children have to understand that your frugal behavior is necessary for the family's financial well-being. Let them know that you want their input for saving money, too. Ask them to help you think of ways to stretch the clothing budget to the maximum.

Give kids the amount you can and are willing to spend on an item. If they insist on something more than what you can afford, let them know they have to pay the difference. If they are old enough to complain, then they are old enough to learn the importance of living within their means. Let them baby-sit, get a paper route, mow a lawn or wash a car.

Try taking your child to comparison shop with you. Show them the difference in prices at the discount stores versus the department store brands.

Give your kids a budget. If they're mature enough to make rational buying decisions, they can decide to spend most of their budget on one videotape that "all the kids at school" have or use it for several items at a discount store. Understand that fitting in is strong peer pressure for them, but emphasize that they are valued for who they are, not what they have and don't buy them things to show your affection. That's a dangerous message. Also explain that the celebrities who lend their names to products for advertising purposes are being paid handsomely for their endorsement. Watch some commercials with them and point out how the message is presented to dupe them into paying for the celebrity's name on the product.

One friend's trick is to buy her children's clothing in the discount stores but to put it in a fashionable department-store bag when she presents it to them. If they think she bought the outfit in a discount store they think it is "cheap," but if it is perceived to come from an expensive store, chances are they will like it. This is a good way to teach them a lesson in marketing—did they like the item when it was in the bag from the expensive store? Why should those feelings change when they learn where it actually came from?

Sooner or later, kids will learn that they're who they are, no matter what they have.

CHAPTER SEVEN

General Money-Saving Tips for Parents

Families can help each other out in a variety of ways with this crazy game of parenting despite the fact that there are no guidebooks that tell us how to raise happy children and no guarantees, either. There are many happy moments, and what parent isn't thrilled to report momentous events, such as the thrill of their first child's birth or the pride from watching their child sing in the school play. But an honest parent will admit that parenting can also be a very trying vocation. Balancing a sense of self amidst family responsibilities can be stressful, or at the very least, challenging. Relatively few of us are prepared for the most difficult job of being a good mom or dad.

There are many times when you feel you need to be alone, with a good book or your own thoughts, or for the indulgent luxury of watching a favorite program uninterrupted. What you wouldn't give for just a few minutes to close your eyes and regroup before tackling the task of appeasing the varied appetites at dinnertime. Other times you crave not solitude but the company of others who understand what day-to-day management of family life is all about. Sometimes you just need to be with others of a kindred spirit to talk about the stresses of dealing with an unreasonable teacher, problems with the dry cleaner or just the morning struggle of dressing a three-year-old who unequivocally announced that all the clothes in his drawer are "yucky." Baby-sitting co-ops, playgroups and mothers' helpers have come to the rescue for me on many occasions. Sharing child care with others is a solution that can give you much-needed time, at little or no cost, to attend to your needs.

SHARING CHILDREN'S TOYS AND CLOTHING

Another kind of creative sharing will help you rid your overflowing closets of decorative picture frames, kites, roller skates and spinning tops. You can clear the garage cluttered with sleds, old bikes, jump ropes and other items that have long since lost their appeal by sending them to greener pastures on the other side of your fence — your neighbors'. The toy box of treasures no longer prized needs to be recycled for someone else's toddler. And all of that "stuff" lying around your house — the Barbie lunchbox, the xylophone and jackets that no longer fit — need to find a new home. Before you give it to Goodwill, throw it in the trash or take it to a consignment shop, look around to your neighbors and friends. Many people in these tough economic times would be grateful for usable hand-me-downs of clothing, household items and playthings.

Neighborhood toy and clothing exchanges are a great way to recycle what you do not need and lend a helping hand to someone who would appreciate your good junk. You, in turn, may find that your own charitable cause will be enhanced with a much-needed desk, tricycle or scout uniform.

CREATIVE SHARING FOR STRESS RELIEF

To relieve the day-to-day stress, parents need to take a break. Husbands and wives need time together, without the kids, to "date" and have fun or discuss important family issues. This might seem impossible with no money to pay a baby-sitter and certainly no "fun fund" to tap into for a movie or prime rib dinner. The picture does not have to be so bleak. In the section that follows, you will see how, with a little creative thinking, you can schedule time for togetherness without spending a fortune.

■ Consider asking a family member — grandparent, sister-in-law or cousin — to take care of your children on a weeknight. Exchange a service or chore. You or your spouse could offer to mow their lawn on Saturday morning (while the other spouse watches the kids) if they provide four hours of care for your kids. Bake an extra tray of lasagna, a ready-to-use dinner, for their weeknight stay. You could walk around the mall with your spouse or sit and have a leisurely cup of coffee, a low-cost but priceless pleasure that allows you time to talk without interruptions. Or schedule your date night for the evening that the library is offering a free program, such as "Around the World in an Armchair," which in our area is a travel film presentation narrated by someone who has visited a tropical island where the brilliant blues magically turn to gold with each sunset and the beaches are graced with the whitest, finest sand. (Before you make a big commitment to exchange family care for a chore, try it for a couple of weeks and if it isn't working out, either person can bow out.)

■ Two neighbors and I took turns watching each other's kids on a regular basis. Three mornings a week, from 10 A.M. until noon, one of us watched while our children played together. It was great because it gave each parent four hours of free time every week. I used my time to go to the grocery store, visit a friend, schedule a doctor's appointment or work on a project. Since we lived only a few houses from each other, it was convenient to walk over, drop my daughter off, and run home to use my two hours — constructively or frivolously. (I must confess, getting a jump-start on a tan was considered a priority on a few summer mornings!) It is amazing what you can accomplish when you have the whole house to yourself. The kids had a ball and the moms had some much-needed time to themselves. It worked out perfectly, because as good friends, we not only shared the kids but also attitudes, interests and evening fun as, additionally, we took turns hosting family dinners on a monthly basis.

■ The Saturday Night Switch is another cost-effective way to go out for the evening without the expense of a baby-sitter. Make arrangements with a good friend or neighbor to go to their house and watch their kids one Saturday a month. On another Saturday, this person will supervise your children in your home. So it isn't too painful, we had a few rules. Kids must be already fed and, most of the time, already in bed, so the hassles were few. Going out at 8:30 P.M. suited us fine, and this arrangement continues to work for both families after more than a year. Another option that has worked well is to have your friend's kids sleep over. No need for the "out" parents to come in early . . . and they can even sleep later in the morning.

■ Start a baby-sitting co-op or baby-sitting pool with a group of parents. In many areas, there are established cooperatives already in operation. Ask around and you will probably find one. If not, you could initiate one with a large group of people who share your parenting philosophies and values. The idea is to establish a baby-sitting exchange for a group of families within a certain geographic area. You earn "credit" by baby-sitting for others in the co-op. Other participants, in turn, watch your children when you need to go out. If you are interested in starting a co-op, advertise in a church bulletin, at the YMCA or in a newspaper classified ad. My sister-in-law just went door-to-door in her neighborhood and shared her co-op ideas with other mothers. Her co-op has twenty families involved. Hold an organizational meeting to establish the group's policies and procedures. Be sure to discuss child-rearing philosophies and practical details such as meals, hours, transportation and sick policies. We assigned the position of record keeper on a rotating basis. The person who functioned in this position arranged for the baby-sitters and totalled everyone's earned credits. In exchange for handling the volunteer position, the record keeper earned extra credit payable in child-care hours. In addition to giving parents a break, I have seen co-ops also function as a social club, play group, clothing and toy exchange and a sewing and craft circle.

■ In the evening, hire a responsible baby-sitter, no matter what the cost. Don't feel bad about doing something that is going to make you feel good. It is for your mental health that you are going out for the evening. In the long run, it is cheaper than staying in and eventually becoming so frustrated that you end up paying for a therapist, who undoubtedly will use your precious money for that prime rib dinner you deserve.

■ On an as-needed basis, arrange for a teenager to come over and give you a break. By taking a brief time out for only a few dollars an hour, you will miss your family and have renewed enthusiasm for them. Use some of your coupon-saving revenues to pay for this well-deserved treat for mom. If you can't afford to pay someone, exchange an hour each day with a neighbor. Suggest to a neighbor, "One week, I will watch all of our kids from 4 P.M. until 5 P.M. and next week it can be your pleasure (your turn!)." What a sanity-saver and no money exchanged!

KEEPING PARENTS IN TOUCH

For fun and parent therapy, why not start a Mommy (or parent) Club. We kiddingly called ours the Make the Most of Your Morning Club. Four parents and their kids is a good size for a group. Set aside one morning a week to meet at the playground armed with a picnic basket filled with drinks, snacks or an easy lunch (don't forget plenty of tissues and a first-aid kit). It is a great way to start off your day. You can even branch out to other places. In season, visit an apple orchard and return home to roll out some apple pies. Our spouses loved that one! Or, sign the group up for the story hour at the library and afterwards treat the kids to an ice-cream cone. Depending on the weather, we selected appropriate activities such as going to a pizza shop, construction site, florist shop, police station, firehouse, pet store, small airport, botanical garden and dairy farm.

There is a group called Moms in Touch. This is a prayer group organized by several mothers with similar interests. They decided to meet and pray for their children, and the teachers and administrators of the public schools they attended. They also send encouragement to the teachers via home-baked cookies and notes of appreciation. They recognize that the teachers are in a position to befriend children who are dealing with many pressures and hope that their prayers will help before a crisis occurs. Specific guidelines for Moms in Touch are available by writing: Moms in Touch, P.O. Box 1163, Poway, CA 92064.

SHARING THE CARING — HOME-BASED BUSINESS

If you need extra income and you love caring for children, you might try to start a small child-care business in your home. Many people do not want to be tied down to caring for a houseful of kids every day. You might consider sharing the day-care business with a compatible partner. To find out all the details about starting a child-care business in the home, I suggest you read my book, *Start Your Own At-Home Child-Care Business*. I wrote this how-to guide after operating my business in which I cared for eleven children in my home — and lived to tell about it! There are many advantages for sharing this type of business in terms of maintaining time for yourself and addressing the concerns of the parents. Day-care providers are fresh and ready to meet the challenges of children when they know they will work one week and have the next week off. At different locations, the kids have different toys and activities giving them the best of both worlds in terms of a variety of games and interests. For example, you may enjoy making crafts with the kids while your partner may love to take the kids on nature walks around the yard searching for feathers and pinecones. A day-care partnership can provide some extra money, without the commitment of a full-time job, in a business that is fun, profitable and relatively easy to start. Of course, it can also be challenging and requires some serious consideration before you jump in.

HOW TO WORK AT HOME FOR PAY

For many parents the idea of working at home sounds idyllic. If you currently work outside of the home, you undoubtedly incur daily expenses like gas, day care, lunches, contributions to the office wedding and shower collections and wardrobe expenses. In addition, someone else is the boss. After the birth of my second baby, I decided to surrender and free myself. I traded business suits for blue jeans. And most important I disengaged myself from traffic jams, performance evaluations and the perilous balancing act of managing work, home and family among the stress and guilt. If you decide to operate a business from your home on a full- or part-time basis, there are many pros . . . and many cons. Like me, you will note a savings in the above-mentioned areas. My expensive lunches with co-workers were replaced with eating the remnants of my daughters' peanut butter and jelly sandwiches. There were no more dry-cleaning bills for silk dresses and the extra charges for suits with pleated skirts because my new at-home fashions consisted of jogging suits and jeans, which were completely wash-and-wear.

If you decide to make the switch, what are some businesses that can be operated from home? How would you begin? If you plan to launch a business, the first step is some soul-searching and analysis. I felt there were four criteria that would make such a business worthwhile. It had to be profitable, emotionally satisfying, fun and home-based so I could be with my children. I decided to start a child-care business in my home. This ultimately led to my writing a book about it, which was published by Doubleday, and thus began my unplanned book-writing career.

Before I decided on the child-care business, I had begun to formulate plans for another venture: a catering business. As I enthusiastically developed my business plan, I dreamed of creating an empire where my meals would be served at elegant, themed dinner parties. I jotted down food preparation guidelines, grocery lists, plans for my cooking days and envisioned picture-perfect parties. I had files filled with recipes for munchies, dips and finger foods. Buffet settings, barbecues and sit-down dinners would be available for those who used my services.

It was my husband who first burst my bubble, and he soon had the strong support of my immediate family. They gently (and not so gently) reminded me that they had only seen or heard of home-cooked meals four times a month in my kitchen, that I have said on many occasions that I hate to cook, and that whenever there is a family picnic, I am asked to bring a centerpiece or a few six-packs of soda rather than anything homemade. They were all quick to remind me of my

Fourth-of-July potato salad that left four relatives who ate it feeling sick. I learned a lesson from their honesty. Decide on the type of work that suits your skills, abilities and interests before investing time and money in a business. Catering would not be in my best interests nor those of my potential clients!

Many books give ideas for businesses that require little or no investment. Beware of the many types of businesses that lure you with the promise of big-time commissions but require a substantial financial investment up-front for supplies and equipment.

My friend was always looking for a way to make easy money. To me, her personality seemed well-suited for accounting and computer work. Her mind was very logical and she loved analytical work. Time and time again, she would fall into the trap of some sort of sales scheme. With each entrepreneurial venture, she plunked down hundreds of dollars that she couldn't afford to lose. Within two years' time, she had started a variety of home-party plans to sell jewelry, toys, water purifiers and expensive makeup. None of them worked out for her, and her garage is now filled with half-opened cartons, sample products and demo kits. The moral of this story is that she was not suited for sales.

Before beginning any business, read about it, talk to people who are actually involved in that field, and ask them the pros and cons of their situations. Take a noncredit course that will teach you the basics of small business startup and operation. Several small business associations offer seminars and helpful information. If you don't know of any in your area, contact your local chamber of commerce, which is sure to have information on these organizations. There are many options for rewarding work that can either be operated in your home, such as a day-care business, or use your home as the base office for services rendered outside the home, such as party-planning services or a clowning business. Some business opportunities my friends and I have considered are listed below along with titles of appropriate how-to books for reference purposes. Try to check these books out of the library first to get a feel for the business, and if you decide to become involved with the idea, purchase the book because you will want to refer to the information as you proceed. If the books you want are not available in your area, request the "Whole Work Catalog," 1515 23rd Street, Box 339-CT, Boulder, CO 80306. All of the books listed below are available by mail-order.

Here are some businesses that can be run from the home:

Moonlighting. If you are not sure where your talents lie but you enjoy dabbling with crafts, auto detailing, house sitting, pool service, furniture refinishing or gift basket design, skim through books that list a variety of part-time jobs. *Moonlighting: 148 Great Ways to Make Money on the Side*, Hausman. Also see *The Teenage Entrepreneur's Guide: 50 Money Making Business Ideas*, Riehm.

Gardening. If you enjoy gardening, grow herbs and garden produce for restaurants and produce stands. *Cash from Square Foot Gardening*, Bartholomew.

Word processing and typing. If you want to use your office skills to enter a lucrative field, read a book that helps you with obtaining start-up money, attracting your customers, pricing your services and tips on professionalism. *Word Processing Profits at Home, A Complete Business Plan*, Glenn; *How to Start a Word Processing Service*, Elman; *How to Make $100,000 a Year in Desktop Publishing*, Williams.

Crafts. If you dream of selling your crafts to shops, co-op shows and party plans, you need someone to share the inside secrets for success. I personally know this author, Barbara Brabec, and her publications are highly recommended. *Creative Cash: How to Sell Your Crafts, Needlework and Know-How* and *Crafts Marketing Success Secrets*. She also has a wonderful newsletter, *National Home Business Report*, available on a subscription basis. For info, write Barbara Brabec, Box 2137 Dept. PG, Naperville, IL 60567.

Child Care. I operated a home-based child-care business on a full-time basis and later ran a Mothers' Day Out program twice a week in my home. Both programs were fun, profitable and suited my need for a supplemental income while providing playmates for my children. I enjoyed meeting lots of new friends—the parents of the children in my program. Details of how to successfully begin and operate child-care programs are described completely in my book, *Start Your Own At-Home Child-Care Business*, $15.95, Box 555, Worcester, PA 19490. Also of interest to anyone who is considering this business are three special publications, *100 Ways to Keep Kids Happy*, *Common Day Care Problems* and *Tips About Organizing Child Care Programs* ($10 for all three publications). Other good resources are *Careers in Child Care*, Visser and Woy, and *Little People: Big Business, A Guide to Successful In-Home Day Care*, Gillis, Sawyer, Kealey and Dempsey-Dubrow.

Literary services. If you like to read and write, offer your services for editing, proofreading, ghostwriting and research. *Careers for Bookworms and Other Literary Types*, Ebert.

Writing. Many people wonder how to break into writing for newspapers and magazines. A freelance writing career is something that definitely can be done from the home. Others would like to get their romance novel, nonfiction howto or children's book published. There are so many books available to help you get off to a good writing start. For inspiration and solid advice about breaking into the writing market, begin with *For All the Write Reasons, Forty Successful Authors, Agents, Writers and Publishers Tell You How to Get Your Book Published*, Gallagher ($24.95), Box 555, Worcester, PA 19490. This is my recently published book that tells all I wish someone had told me when I began. Once you're done writing something and are ready to sell it, *Writer's Market*, published by Writer's Digest Books, is an essential reference.

Photography. Amateurs and pros alike can make money with a camera. Sporting events, schools, dance recitals and animal shows are all potential markets for you to begin a profitable business that requires little investment and allows you to devote as much time as you want to it. Shooting photos for all types of occasions is explained in *How You Can Make $25,000 a Year With Your Camera*, Cribb.

Beauty Consulting. This is a tricky one. You must really be sure this is your area of expertise. A friend of mine recently went into this business. Her decision shocked many people! She spends little time on makeup, wardrobe and beauty routines and does not, in my opinion, have the image herself that would inspire confidence with clients who want advice about improving their appearance. Another friend has done this successfully for years. She looks the part, and her customers look to her for advice on colors, wardrobe and makeup. To learn the ins and outs of starting an image-consulting business, read *Image Consulting*, Timberlake.

Clowning. Birthday party clowns are popular in our area. For a forty-five-minute presentation, the clowns are paid $75. Clowns also make appearances at company picnics and grand-opening events. The inside scoop about a home-based clowning business is explained in the guide, *Creative Clowning*, Fife.

Flea Markets and Antiques. If you have a scrounger gene in you, this can be a profitable part-time business. You need to have a sense of what items you should buy and resell later. To learn how to start with a minimum investment, read *How to Make a Living in Antiques*, Ketchum; *Flea Market Finds*, Werner; and *How to Make Cash Money at Swap Meets, Flea Markets, Etc.*, Cooper.

Cleaning. Yes, there really are some people who like to do windows! This business requires little start-up capital but a real know-how for cleaning. If you operate it truly like a business, watching your time and quality, cleaning a few houses a week can be quite profitable. A few helpful sources are *Cleaning Up for a Living*, Aslett; *How to Start a Window Cleaning Business*, Suvall; and *How to Start a Cleaning and Janitorial Service*, Frances.

Other businesses to consider include mowing lawns, using your van or pickup to haul away unwanted junk, real estate, making gift baskets, cooking and baking, pet-sitting, consulting in your area of expertise, a temporary-employment agency, landscape design, tending other people's gardens, an errand-running service, repair services, gift-buying service, adult day care, caring for handicapped while their primary caretaker takes a break, a grocery shopping service, a household organizing service, a chauffeur service, publicist, a meal-delivery service, sewing or mending, interior design, a tutoring service for children or adults or teaching a language. As you brainstorm with friends and family, you will come up with an idea that is right for you. Be cautious of the promises of franchises and various party plans. They are usually very expensive and may not be in business to serve you down the road. Attend a reputable franchise show and thoroughly research any franchise before plunking down a sizeable investment.

No matter which business you research, part of your preliminary education should include readings such as *How to Set Up and Operate Your Office From Home*, Scott; *Working From Home* and *The One Hundred Best Home-Based Businesses for the Nineties*, Edwards; *Homemade Money*, Brabec; *Surviving the Start-up Years in Your Own Business*, Marder; and *Stay Home and Mind Your Own Business*, Frohbiefer-Mueller.

CHAPTER EIGHT

Miscellaneous Savings Around the House

J ust about the time you feel you finally have a grasp on your bills and budget, you can count on being walloped with a major car bill. The expenses associated with gas, oil, car payments, insurance and registration are anticipated and to some degree palatable, though not entirely agreeable. A major auto repair is always a shock to the budget. The advice that follows gives common-sense shortcuts to automobile well-being and practical suggestions for keeping your car in tip-top condition.

SAVINGS ON CAR MAINTENANCE

The advice of the professionals is to always take care of the basics in order to keep major breakdowns minimal. The problem with such advice is that routine care is not affordable for many families. Sure, it would be nice to prevent major troubles before they inconvenience you, but in reality, checking the cooling system and replacing that old, dirty oil costs money. In theory, we all know it makes sense, but for many people that leftover $50 in the checking account has a list of multiple causes putting in a claim.

There are many easy-to-learn, do-it-yourself procedures that can add to your car's life expectancy and save you money, thus adding to your *wheels of fortune*, too. A friend of mine asked a neighborhood mechanic if she could look over his shoulder while he worked on her car. He looked at her like she had eight heads but agreed. She asked lots of why-and-how questions and in the process learned some effective checkup techniques to maintain her car.

Professional advice should be sought before embarking on any long-distance trips. It is prudent to have a mechanic give your car a once-over inspection. Traveling in a car filled with kids arguing about which tape to play and dealing with car sickness, a squirmy dog and suitcases overflowing the car-top carrier is stressful enough. If you can lessen the possibilities of minor irritations, such as malfunctioning wiper blades, or the probability of a major disaster, such as the jerking feeling of a failing transmission on an interstate highway, you will be doing yourself a tremendous favor. The final straw is when your car must be towed on a holiday weekend and repaired by an unknown mechanic you may not trust!

The best advice I can share is to establish a good relationship with an independent mechanic who is not affiliated with a dealership. In the past, we had service performed by the dealership where the car was purchased. Even for minor problems, the repair costs were staggering. The first routine maintenance for a six-month-old car cost us $323. Especially frustrating was the fact that we had paid for an extended-service warranty, but still most "routine maintenance" items were not included.

Check with several friends, neighbors and used-car dealers for the name of the garage they use. Asking one person isn't really the best way. When several people feel a mechanic does quality work, reliably, at a fair price, then consider that person. When you interview a prospective mechanic (before you actually need an emergency repair), ask if the work is guaranteed, if he provides an itemized bill for all parts and labor costs, if towing locally is available, and if you can take it for a short test drive before you pay for it and drive it home (only to find out that what you paid to have fixed still buzzes, clatters or screeches when you go up a hill). A friend recommended our mechanic, who has saved the day for us on many occasions. We trust him to make the necessary repairs on our van and station wagon, and if it isn't broken, he doesn't fabricate a repair bill. A mechanic you trust can save you hundreds of dollars per year.

And by now, you know that I like to barter. Once not long ago, my husband, an accountant, did taxes in exchange for some body work our car needed. Think of your talents, interests and hobbies. You might offer baby-sitting, lawn care, a fence installation, word processing, some public relations work, or a few home-cooked meals for your mechanic's family. Don't pay full price if you can arrange a mutually beneficial trade.

These are some things you can accomplish with the aid of your owner's manual, a lesson from a garage mechanic, an adult night course or a quick study of a book from the library on automobile maintenance:

■ Replace headlights, taillights and wiper blades.

■ Check for worn tires, bald spots, inadequate tread.

■ Fill tires with air (then do your best to avoid potholes, broken glass in the road and parking too close to a curb).

■ Make sure you have a spare tire and the proper tools to change a tire.

■ Practice changing a tire before you find yourself caught unprepared with a real need to do just that.

■ Know how to check the important fluids in your car and how to fill the car with oil, transmission fluid, antifreeze, wiper fluid and water as needed.

■ Check under the hood for any wires that look frayed or worn.

■ Check hoses for cracks.

■ Eyeball your car and make sure nothing is dangling from the underside of the vehicle.

Here are some things to do right now, with no special skills.

■ Put together an emergency equipment box that contains owner's service manual, rope, jumper cables, flares, instant tire inflator, small fire extinguisher, tools, spare tire, car jack, lug wrench, a few dollars for the unexpected, first-aid kit, paper, pen, flashlight, funnel, empty container to fill with gas if you run out before you find the next station, white flag, reflective warning triangles, flares for dense fog, rags, handkerchief to signal an emergency, map, nonperishable snacks and drinks (you may be waiting in the car longer than you ever dreamed possible!).

■ Make sure you have your driver's license, insurance card, owner's registration card and emergency phone numbers.

■ Because many newer vehicles today are digitally controlled, leaving the big repair jobs to the experts is a wise move. It is not prudent to tackle a job beyond your mechanical abilities. You may have to pay someone to undo the damages you inflicted upon the car.

■ For routine maintenance, follow the recommended repair schedule, which is given to you when you buy the car. (Tell the mechanic that you do not want him to proceed with any work until you okay the estimate. Some people insist upon a written estimate of what is to be done and the cost.)

■ Read the owner's manual for tips about fuel savings and car maintenance. For example: You will use less gas if you have less weight in the trunk, so empty out the extras in the trunk! Save gas and wear and tear by combining trips and errands. Obey the speed limit — going faster uses more fuel. Don't believe everything you read or hear; many gas-saving gadgets are just that — gadgets that don't do what they promise.

■ Have the oil changed regularly.

■ Get a tune-up at scheduled intervals.

■ Carpool, bike, walk or use public transportation to reduce the wear and tear of your car.

■ Check the community, shopping center or office bulletin boards for potential carpool arrangements — travel off-peak hours on public transportation if the fare is lower.

■ Inquire if there is a radio call-in show that deals with automotive issues.

Money-saving tips are always welcome, so keep these in mind when you are trying to cut corners.

■ Don't buy oil at the gas station — you can buy it cheaper by the case when you see a sale at a discount store.

■ Pump your own gas if self-serve is less expensive.

■ Wash and wax your own car, buy upholstery shampoo and do your own interior detailing.

- Only use premium gasoline if it will really make a difference in your car's performance (ask a knowledgeable mechanic for an expert opinion).
- Comparison-shop for gasoline prices.
- Go to the station that is convenient and saves you the most per gallon.
- Use cash instead of a credit card if a discount is earned for cash.
- Use a credit card to pay a repair bill. In case there is a dispute, you can contact the credit card company and delay paying the charge until resolved.
- Check with your insurance agent about coverage that includes car rental and towing costs in case you need these services. I have had to pay for these expensive items out of pocket and later found out that this coverage was available for only a modest increase in the premium.
- Use carpet samples as car floor mats for those snowy days to absorb the water and keep your car clean. You can even spray them with a carpet or fabric protector so they resist stains.

Consider joining an auto club. It gives you a sense of security if you belong to a group that provides around-the-clock emergency road service. Emergency towing and roadside service for a flat tire and fuel delivery have been reassuring to me on more occasions than I would like to admit. They also offer booklets that give advice on purchasing new and used cars. However, if you do not travel often and live in a climate where rain and snow are rare, you may not need the service. Inquire about the benefits of a full-service club or limited-service club. If the membership fee is minimal, you may want to participate for the emergency road service and the ancillary benefits such as travel planning, road maps and advice about best routes, etc.

Contact the local AAA office (the phone number is listed in the Yellow Pages) and ask for a free copy of the "AAA Gas Watcher's Guide." To receive a free copy by mail, send a #10 self-addressed stamped envelope to AAA Gas Watcher's Guide, Mail Stop 150, 1000 AAA Drive, Heathrow, FL 32746-5063.

Contact the Superintendent of Documents, Government Printing Office, Washington, DC 20402, for helpful booklets about domestic and foreign auto manufacturers.

Ask your local Shell service station for a booklet titled "The Gas Mileage Book" or request in writing from: Shell Gas Mileage Book, Box 61609, Houston, TX 77208.

Warranties and extended-service contracts available for purchase are not all-inclusive. There seem to be many loopholes, and cases argued for and against their value depend on the experiences you've had. But sometimes you do get lucky and hear those words near and dear to your heart, "That will be covered by your warranty." (Maybe once in this person's lifetime!) For further information on warranties and service contracts, request a fact sheet from the Public Reference Department, Federal Trade Commission, Washington, DC 20580.

Before coughing up your hard-earned cash for a repair, read the warranty or, better yet, call the manufacturer. Make an attempt to determine if the problem is covered by your service policy. Don't rely on the mechanic to tell you if it is.

If you have had a problem with an auto manufacturer that has not been resolved to your satisfaction, contact the U.S. Consumer Product Safety Commission, (800) 638-8326.

Try calling a vocational technical school that has an auto mechanic program. My cousin has always been a whiz at car repairs. Even in tenth grade he could determine what was wrong with a car and fix it. His high school vo-tech school was available to our community for some repair jobs. It was great work experience, good on-the-job training for the students and a break in car-repair expenses for us. If you feel really "brave," ask the teacher if the students would like to "borrow" your car for a few days so they can really look it over for you, do needed repairs and gain additional practice.

ALTERNATE WAYS TO COMMUNICATE LONG-DISTANCE WITH LOVED ONES

Unfortunately, with corporate mergers and high unemployment, many families today are transient. They must move to locations where they can find work in order to provide for their families. Relatives who used to live around the corner from each other are forced to move to distant cities. This causes many people to feel isolated. It is comforting to be able to pick up the phone and call a loved one after you have had a tough day at work or home. Their voice often reassures you that things will get better and that they have felt that way too. Urgent news, such as the loss of a first tooth, the rabbit that won't come out from under the car, the gerbil that had babies or a career change in progress, are screaming to be recounted over the long-distance wire service. Staying in touch to share the day-to-day joys and sorrows of family life is desirable, but difficult sometimes at long-distance rates. Reaching out and touching someone (at any carrier's rates) can add a significant amount to the phone charges each month.

Here are some projects you can adopt to keep in contact with your friends and family who live miles away.

1. My daughter is the family "General News" newsletter editor. Relatives send her little bits of information as they happen. Throughout the month, scribble-scrabble artwork, typewritten stories and handwritten notes arrive in our mailbox recounting the events important to our family nationwide. I address the envelopes and Kristen decorates them with markers and stickers. Now with newsletter number seven in progress, we have even added a special recipe section that includes the particulars for Rice Krispies marshmallow treats, Rice

Chex cereal party mixes, Jell-O Jigglers and directions for making peanut butter play dough.

2. Progressive letters are fun too. In our family, it works like this. My brother's family begins the letter by telling about the highlights in their family life. After including news about school talent shows, birthdays, upcoming events, interesting trips and achievements, the letter is passed along to the next family. They add their tidbits and it continues. The last family, in this case mine, is responsible for making copies and sending a finished copy of the progressive letter to each family. This progressive letter, now in its third year, strengthens family ties and brings a feeling of family unity despite the physical distance that separates us. Don't panic, this is only done about twice a year!

3. Read your junk mail. I never thought I would advocate such a thing but occasionally a long-distance telephone carrier offers a special rate that can save you money. You could set aside an off-peak time to call your relatives when the rates are at their lowest. So you don't forget any of the family highlights, jot them down as they happen and post on the refrigerator or near the phone. Then in the excitement of trying to fill everyone in on the news, check to see that your main points and interesting anecdotes are included in the conversation.

4. If you have a photograph to send to relatives, take it to a quick-print shop and see how it copies on the enlargement setting. Then use the reverse side to write your letter. Color copiers now available are also fun to try.

5. If you need the comfort of a phone call but want to limit your call to three minutes, set a kitchen timer that will buzz when time is up. You can always choose to ignore it. This can be especially helpful if several people need to be included in rotating conversations. By setting a timer, everyone gets a fair amount of time to relate their news. It is also an effective method to limit the amount of time teens are allowed to talk on the phone. Give them a limit on phone use per night. They may make or receive one call or several — the choice is theirs. Many bills today are based on message unit rates and even local calls can run up your family phone bill.

6. When my aunt's grandchildren lived in California and she resided in Pennsylvania, she bridged the mileage gap by reading nursery rhymes and favorite stories into a tape recorder. She then sent the tapes to her grandchildren. Her renditions of *Goodnight Moon* and *Where the Wild Things Are* were enjoyed night after night. It became part of the bedtime routine to listen to Grandma's voice telling them to cuddle up with their blanket, close their eyes and she would read them a story. They, too, sent her weekly tapes that told what they did each day and who their friends were. Their mother turned the tape recorder on to capture special times like opening the Christmas presents, nursery school graduation and preparations for the Easter bunny.

7. My mother makes her own storybook tapes for her grandchildren — com-

plete with her own "signal," a bell, for when it is time to turn the page. She buys a favorite book, reads a story or favorite fairy tale into the cassette player and rings a little bell to indicate when it is time to turn the page. She wraps up the book and cassette and mails a package to the three families with grandchildren. Last week we received *Lady and the Tramp*, and as a Christmas gift our family received *101 Dalmatians*.

8. A picture is worth a thousand words. Watching a videotape that captures in animated living color the family vacation at the beach or a first birthday party is a priceless way to keep in touch. If you don't own a videocamera, borrow or rent one for a few hours. Barter with a friend and ask them to film your special event, and you in turn will offer to help them with something. Receiving a video of the grandchildren would be a real treat for a long-distance grandparent — and vice versa.

9. Surprise letters can be spontaneous notes that you jot down as a young child dictates their words to you. The child decorates the letter, puts it in an envelope and mails it to a relative. And do you really need all of the artwork that comes home from school? Send a few of those test papers marked with "job well done" and a finger painting or two to a loved one. (You can get rid of a little clutter on your refrigerator that way, too!) Or, flip them over and let the kids write thank-you notes. Great low-cost stationery! What a pleasant surprise for the chosen recipient.

10. Collect odds and ends from the mail and free offers found on and in cereal boxes. Stock up on flower seeds, trial sizes of cereal, and items on special sale tables. Kids love to receive mail, so every once in a while send coloring books, a whistle, fancy straws, fun games, decals, stickers, coupons for pizza and booklets to your cousins and friends. You can even help each other start a stamp collection. Collect stamps from your mail and trade the exotic and not-so-exotic stamps through the mail.

11. Granddaddy isn't much of a letter-writer but he loves to keep in touch with his eleven grandchildren with postcards. He keeps a stack of them in his office desk, regularly jots a note, riddle or love message on one, and pops it in the mail. Kids love to get mail and it is an easy way for him to keep in touch. Before our recent trip to visit, he sent postcards to the kids who were going with a count-down of the number of days until the trip and some clues about some of the sur-prises he had waiting for them.

12. My parents regularly send their grandchildren sample products they re-ceive in the mail such as shampoo, individual hot chocolate envelopes, tooth-paste and cereal. While traveling, they collect complimentary sugar, soap, snacks and shower caps from hotel rooms. We are also the recipients of a $10 bill about once a month with a coupon they clipped out for fast food. A little note says sim-ply, "Take the kids out for lunch."

Telephone Tips

■ Use 800 or toll-free numbers whenever possible to order through a catalog or call for any type of information. Call the 800 information number at (800) 555-1212, and ask the directory assistance operator if the company or organization you wish to reach has an 800 number. If you are unable to find the 800 number via directory assistance, contact the local branch office of the company or organization and ask to speak to Consumer Affairs, Public Relations or Customer Service. They may be able to connect you through their company phone lines. Then you won't have to pay for the long-distance call. If you want to order a useful directory that lists 800 numbers for a variety of companies and organizations, call (800) 426-8686. Inquire about the current price for their business- or consumer-oriented directory.

■ For a list of travel-related services that offer 800 numbers, send $2 to Scott American Company, Box 88, West Redding, CT 06896. Many hotels, car rental companies, vacation travel companies and tourist information services offer 800 numbers that are included on this list.

■ Don't use 900 numbers to enter a contest, give your opinion or use a service. There is a hefty cost associated with such calls. I have a friend who was thrilled to receive an announcement in the mail stating that she had won a contest. The instruction was to call the 900 number listed and she would receive her prize. She was connected, put on hold, forced to listen to a long recorded advertising message — and all the while the clock kept ticking and her phone bill increased. A $50 charge had accrued for the four calls she made trying to claim a prize that never materialized.

Read your horoscope in the paper. It is no doubt as accurate as the astrologer on the other end of the 900 number.

■ Did you know you have to pay for directory-assistance calls? I am always surprised when I see how many unnecessary calls I made for telephone number information because the phone book was not conveniently located (and I was too lazy to try to find it). Keep a small book close to the phone with frequently called numbers to avoid these costs.

■ Check your phone bill each month to make sure you have not been charged for any calls you did not make. Be sure that you are not being charged for any extra services. If you do not use call forwarding or three-way calling, eliminate the services because the charges are significant over a period of time.

■ If you misdial a long-distance or toll number, report it to the operator so you will not be billed for the wrong number dialed.

HOW TO SAVE MONEY ON UTILITIES

Other than turning lights out when not in use and fixing leaky faucets, are there ways to significantly reduce utility costs? Last year, we made a concerted effort to cut our energy bills. I researched how we could achieve major savings by following all the energy guru's advice about insulating our home, maintaining our appliances economically and using weather stripping and caulking to seal around windows and doors. The result was a warm, cozy home.

Read books in the library about cutting your energy bills. The time spent in reading books, articles, consumer magazines and energy columns about how to deflate skyrocketing fuel costs is a wise investment. There are energy-inspection services listed in the Yellow Pages. Many offer in-home evaluations and can give specific recommendations for your home. You can troubleshoot and discover many hidden air infiltration and energy leaks on your own. Sometimes, helpful information and free home evaluations are available from the utility companies themselves. Call the customer service office and make some inquiries.

Energy-Saving Tips

■ Have a family meeting and ask for suggestions from the troops about how, with some team effort and cooperation, the household could conserve energy. You may need to have a "training seminar" to instill the value of closing the doors, not running the water while brushing teeth, turning off the television when not in use, closing windows, not using the shower as a means to wake up, and turning the lights out after use. Assign one person to read the water and electric meter in the morning and in the evening, and chart how much electricity you use per day or week. Compare your energy bills from one month to the next. Make up some sort of game to try to reduce the household's daily energy consumption. If everyone puts forth their best effort and you notice you have saved a significant amount over last year's same-month bill, splurge and do something special for the family.

■ Contact your utility companies and ask for booklets about energy-saving tips. The tips offered will be different according to your location because of the variety of climate, different types of heating and cooling systems and fuel rates in your locale. You may want to ask for customer information or the public relations department. Your gas utility company, for example, might suggest reducing the setting on your hot water heater, allowing the system to operate without using as much energy to heat the water, thus saving you money.

■ Use a portable heater to warm up one room. Do not use a kerosene or space heater if you have small children or a pet that may touch it or knock it over.

■ Use a nightlight in the hallway instead of keeping the bathroom light on for the kids. For years, we used a full-wattage ceiling bulb all night long. We finally got the "bright idea" to use a rabbit night-light that plugs into the hall wall socket. A friend suggested painting the doorknob of the hall bathroom with fluorescent paint so people can find their way without a light on. Or paint a piece of masking tape with a fluorescent color and attach to any significant landmarks for nightwalkers.

■ Ask your neighbors and friends how they save money on energy costs. Since all of the houses in our development are built basically the same, we can learn from each other. One neighbor insulated a crawl space, another insulated the basement, a third started with insulating the walls and the fourth bought an insulated covering at the hardware store to wrap the hot water heater. We were advised to invest in attic insulation, which saved us a bundle the very first winter. Plug areas with weather stripping anywhere air leaks in, and insulate wherever possible.

■ Storm windows and doors require a cash outlay, but they do save on energy consumption. Watch for any cracks in the storm windows and replace or repair. If you cannot afford to buy storm windows for the entire house at once, perhaps you could buy a few windows each season or buy them all at the end of winter when they are on sale. If you do not have small children, you could fabricate your own storm windows by securely attaching clear, heavy plastic over windows to eliminate cold drafts. Use masking tape to attach plastic to the windows. Small children, at least mine anyway, "popped" the plastic on their bedroom windows within two days of installation. Also, plastic of any type can be dangerous for young children, who can easily suffocate.

■ You may not be able to afford to weather barrier the whole house with insulation, but by plugging where you can, savings will be noted. Many home-improvement centers offer seminars on weatherproofing homes. Their information nights are designed, of course, to sell their products. You may decide to purchase their materials, but most important, you will learn the correct level of thickness for insulation in your area, recommended safety precautions when insulating and some helpful shortcuts and timesaving methods for installation.

■ Go through your house, room by room, including the attic and basement, and note any cracks or repairs needed to keep out water or cold air.

■ Keep heating vents dirt-free and bug-free because any obstruction will prevent proper circulation of your system's warm winter air or cool summer air. You may feel that the system is not on high enough and rush to adjust the thermostat when the problem isn't the temperature setting but clogged vents.

■ Weatherproof your window air conditioner by covering it so cold air doesn't come through during the winter months when it is not used.

■ Ask your local utility if the rates are lower for usage during off-peak hours. If it costs less to run your appliances at night, then that's the time you should run them. Peak hours may be different in the summer than in the winter months, so check with the utility companies in your area.

■ Hang wash on the line to air dry and save on the electricity consumed by the dryer. Remove clothes from a dryer as soon as they are finished to save on ironing time and associated electric costs. My mother-in-law used a wooden clothes rack to dry her clothes. She never had a dryer and just used the rack in the basement near the heater.

■ Keep your appliances in good condition to save money by operating them efficiently. When it is time to replace them, shop for energy-efficient appliances. It's safe to assume energy costs will increase, so it's smart to shop for energy-savers.

■ If you install a new toilet, ask about the low-flush models that use less water per flush than the standard types. One family saved 15,000 gallons of water in a year.

■ Use washers and dishwashers for full loads only if you really want to be energy efficient. Personally, I almost laughed as the salesperson demonstrated the small-load setting on my washing machine. Who raising a normal family ever does a small load? As you can imagine, the small-load setting hasn't been touched since we were in the store, but I guess it's nice to know we have one.

■ Replace filters in your home's heater according to the manufacturer's operating manual. Dust and dirt accumulate, and the heater requires more energy to do the same job.

■ Empty the lint catcher in your dryer after each load. If you neglect to do this, clothes will take longer to dry, using more energy and thus increasing the cost to you. Clean the coils behind the refrigerator for the same energy-saving reason.

■ Hot water costs a lot of money. Eliminating twenty-minute showers and replacing them with a twenty-minute soak in the bathtub may reduce costs. Also, there are special shower nozzles available at hardware stores that allow less water to spray through, thus conserving water and money spent on water costs.

■ Ask the family members to shorten their time in the shower. Any possibility of four-minute showers if you promise to read a story or play a game with the kids if they get out before the timer goes off?

■ Repair leaky faucets so your hard-earned income does not go down the drain. The accumulation of drips over a period of time can easily add up to the cost of a dinner, VCR or weekend away. Don't let your money literally go down the drain.

■ Lower the thermostat at night and bundle up. Buy flannel sheets and pillowcases for a comfortable feeling. Sophisticated programmable thermostats make it easy to cut back the temperature settings both at night and during the day in houses that are unoccupied for most of the day.

■ Plant shade trees near the windows if you want your home to stay cool. Trees will block the hot sun from streaming into a room and cut air-conditioning costs. Use awnings, drapes or blinds to reduce the sun's glare. If you can't afford air conditioning, ceiling fans can stir up a nice breeze in any room. They are not expensive and add a nice decorative touch.

■ Check your monthly bills. Computers can make errors in billing. If something doesn't look right, question it.

Safety tip: Get rid of any old, inefficient or dangerous appliances. A fire could start. Check your smoke alarms frequently. If they are the battery-operated type, replace batteries as needed.

PERSPECTIVES ON POTIONS

Oh, sure, you can spend your hard-earned money on pine-oil disinfectants, toilet bowl cleaners and clogged drain products that beckon for purchase on alluring television commercials, and the packaging is pretty neat-looking, too. But, what a sense of satisfaction you can gain (and save real cents too!) when you say, "Wait, there are alternatives." Many people save money by using homemade formulas to make their own cleaning products. This creates a safer household environment as well. Simple, old-fashioned compounds of rubbing alcohol, ammonia, soap flakes, baking soda and white vinegar are still effective and remain the basis of many commercial cleaners. It takes just a few minutes of your time to whip up your own back-to-nature cleaners that cost a fraction of their comparable store-bought products.

In the days of our great-grandparents, homemade household potions were the only choices. They worked well then and are effective now. I advocate whenever possible to return to using some of these chemical-free choices that save money and, in many cases, help the environment, too. Reducing the output of chemicals and cutting down on wasteful commercial packaging makes the environment safer for all families. There are many alternative uses for everyday items that, used in a new way, can save you money. (Did you know you can remove a ballpoint pen stain by saturating the spot with hairspray and then washing it out with warm water?)

How can you begin, how long does it take to concoct the less-expensive alternatives, and is it worth the trouble? As you look over the commonplace ingredients, you will get into the habit of thinking like a penny-pinching parent because many of the ingredients are already in your kitchen cabinet. It is worth it to mix-it-up as most ingredients are easy to find and economical to buy. And when you succeed at saving money by implementing these ideas, pass the ideas along and share them with other parents who would appreciate saving a few extra dollars.

Browse through flea markets, bookstores, libraries and estate sales for old cookbooks, gardening books, medical books, etc. In such treasures you will find old-fashioned formulas, information and recipes that once were passed along from generation to generation but now are in danger of being lost forever on some

---

Good reading for household tips:

Stepping Lightly on the Earth: Everyone's Guide to Toxics in the Home. For a copy, write to Greenpeace, 1436 U Street, NW, Washington, DC 20009. You will find several recipes for natural cleansers.

"Polly's Pointers," the popular syndicated column, offers a copy of a newsletter entitled "Cleaning with Vinegar and Baking Soda" for $1.25. Send to Polly's Pointers, in care of *Raising Happy Kids on a Reasonable Budget*, Box 93863, Cleveland, OH 44101-5863.

The *Rodale's Book of Practical Formulas* includes lots of easy-to-make, easy-to-use recipes (1991 edition).

Herbal Medicine, a book by Dian Dincin Buchman, is filled with natural ways to get well and stay healthy.

---

yellowing pages. Recipes for organic fertilizers, hives remedies, eye ointments and liquid soaps are all buried in the pages of these valuable although not scientific papers. It is fun to experiment with making the numerous household formulas. Be sure to follow these guidelines for safety:

Caution 1. Read all labels on cleaning products carefully before using. Many products when combined with others give off hazardous gases. For example, products made with chlorine should never be mixed with products containing ammonia. Do not mix a large quantity of cleaner at any one time. Squirt cleaning bottles are tempting for a child's sense of exploration.

Caution 2. Label the cleansers if they are in new containers and keep all products out of the reach of children. Accidental poisonings occur in households with homemade products as well as heavy-duty commercial products. Never allow children to help you mix these formulas for old-fashioned remedies. Warn children that they must never touch these products no matter what they look like or smell like.

Caution 3. Avoid smoking or flames when working with cleaning supplies. Work with windows open and in a well-ventilated room.

Caution 4. Wear rubber gloves to protect your hands when handling ingredients that may irritate the skin.

Caution 5. Thoroughly clean one container before using it for another purpose. The residue of one detergent bottle mixed with the ingredients for a new cleaning agent could cause an adverse reaction. Fumes are dangerous to inhale but a cleaning product splashed on the body can cause serious burns. Ingestion of any cleaning agent is a very serious matter. Any chlorine bleach product bottle should never be near a product that contains acid.

Note: Call the Poison Control Center and request literature about child-proofing your home against accidental poisonings and what to do in chemical emergencies. Your hospital or pediatrician can give you that phone number. Keep it posted next to every phone in your house.

Household Money-Savers

■ It is hard to know if *low-priced cleansers and detergents* mean low quality. Some large containers are mostly water, so how do you decide which to buy? I suggest buying the inexpensive brand as a "trial." If it does the job efficiently with no ill effects, I would continue to buy it.

■ Save slivers of soap from the soap dish and the tiny remainders of any bar of soap to make your own *soft soap*. Grind them up to a fine powder consistency in a food processor or blender. Put them in a pretty pump type or squeeze top container. Add a little bit of water. Voilá! Your very own liquid soft soap. For a more scented soap, add a few drops of perfume. You could put it in a pretty container saved from the store-bought variety for which you paid a few premium dollars before you found out you could make your own "goo." If the solution hardens, add boiling water to soften.

■ Another version of your own *soft soap* is made by cutting up a bar of your favorite scented soap into eight pieces. Fill a saucepan with a quart of water and add the pieces of soap. Cook on low heat until the soap has melted. Add four teaspoons of glycerin, which can be purchased inexpensively from the drugstore. Remove the mixture from the stove and allow to cool before pouring it into individual containers. If the mixture hardens, just add hot water and shake about twenty seconds until it returns to soft-soap consistency.

■ An inexpensive way to clean the oven without using a costly and caustic commercial *oven cleaner* (and the noxious fumes) is to pour one-half cup of ammonia into a cup and place it inside the oven (hopefully one that is not too grimy and grease-filled!). Be sure the oven door is closed tightly. Allow the ammonia to sit overnight, about twelve hours. Then, wipe the interior of the oven with a rag, some mild dishwashing detergent and hot water. Rinse with clear water to add sparkle. This method costs less than the store-bought oven cleaner, and is quite effective.

■ Keep your refrigerator free of rotting food. Keep an open box of baking soda in the refrigerator to *absorb odors* as they occur. Replace it every few months.

■ For a homemade *air deodorant spray*, mix 3 teaspoons of baking soda with 3 cups of water in a spray bottle and spray around the musty or offensive-smelling area. Or put leftover lemon and orange peels to good use. Place them around the room for a fresh scent.

■ *Eliminate foul smells* by mixing ½ ounce borax with allspice, ground cinnamon, whole cloves, nutmeg, ground orrisroot and a cup and a half of lemon and orange peels. Put the mixture in a glass jar with holes poked in the lid so the fragrance can pass through the room.

■ Two tablespoons of citronella, which can be purchased at the pharmacy, mixed with a gallon of water and one-half cup of rubbing alcohol helps to get rid of pet smells. This *pet-odor remover* is very effective. To deter the pet from returning to that spot, wash the area with equal parts of water and vinegar solution.

■ To *remove unpleasant* smells in the refrigerator or elsewhere, place a bowl of white vinegar in the area and the unpleasant odors will be absorbed.

■ For acrylic *floor wax*, many experienced housecleaners have told me to only use half of what is recommended on the bottle by the manufacturer. Try it. If the floor looks just as shiny to you, continue to do it that way and get twice as much for your money.

■ My mother's favorite dollar stretcher is her method for *cleaning glass* areas such as mirrors, windows and glass tabletops. Mix three tablespoons of lemon juice, such as ReaLemon, with a gallon of water. Use newspapers or white gift-wrapping tissue paper instead of rags or paper towels and rub until it is clean. No streaks, beautiful results and very low cost.

■ Another alternative is to mix rubbing alcohol and water in a handy spray bottle for window and glass jobs.

■ The homemade *glass cleaner* that is closest to the store brands is a mixture of a half cup of "sudsy" ammonia, a pint of 70 percent isopropyl rubbing alcohol, one teaspoon liquid dishwashing detergent and enough water to fill a gallon container.

■ For *windows and mirrors*, mix a half cup of white vinegar with a quart of cool water. Use also on fixtures and countertops.

■ Try a handful of cornstarch mixed in a bucket of lukewarm water. Wash *windows and mirrors* and wipe dry.

■ My father recommends buying a large container of windshield wiper cleaner, found in a supermarket or car supply store, for use in *glass cleaning*.

■ Homemade *eyeglass cleaner*? My neighbor mixes 8 ounces of ammonia and 32 ounces of denatured alcohol in a spray bottle.

■ Another old standby for *window and glass cleaner* is a quart of water mixed with one-quarter cup vinegar.

■ With any *glass cleaners*, use sparingly to avoid streaks. Wipe away streaks with a damp towel.

■ *Clean brass* that is tarnished with a lemon rind dipped in salt. For copper items, rub with salt and real lemon juice made into an abrasive-consistency paste. It is important to rub with a soft cloth and rinse thoroughly. Dry to a shine. Also try a paste of flour, vinegar and salt, applied with a clean rag to copper surfaces. Let it stay for an hour or so and wipe clean.

■ For the *vinyl wallpaper* in my kitchen and painted wall areas of my home that are decorated daily with grimy little handprints, food stains and miscellaneous marks, I use a sudsy solution made with 4 tablespoons of a dishwashing liquid, 2 cups of borax (found in the detergent section of the supermarket) and warm water. Rinse with a solution of borax and clean water.

■ Or for *painted walls*, use 2 ounces of borax, 1 teaspoon of ammonia and 2 quarts of water. (Remember to keep all cleaning solutions out of the reach of children and do a test area on a hidden spot before you tackle a spot in the main focus of the wall.)

■ Grease spots on *wallpaper* can usually be removed by mixing cornstarch and water to a paste consistency. Apply the cornstarch paste to the spot, allow to dry and wipe it off. Do a test area first.

■ Toothpaste is good for cleaning *crayon marks* on walls. A small amount of this gentle, abrasive cleaner rubbed and worked into the area, and washed with a damp sponge, works well in removing the colored marks from a painted or papered wall without damaging the surface. (Do a test spot on wallpaper before trying it on the real spot.)

■ Just mix white vinegar and warm water in equal parts in a plastic squirt or spray bottle for quick cleanups around the *kitchen and bathroom*.

■ My mother swears by her *all-purpose cleaner* made by mixing 2 cups rubbing alcohol, 1 tablespoon hand-washing dishwashing liquid (very important: do not use the kind made for automatic dishwashers as this product mixed with ammonia could be dangerous), 2 teaspoons ammonia and a half-gallon water.

■ My friend, whose immaculate home could pass any white-glove test, uses a dishwashing liquid for most of her cleaning needs. She dilutes it with water and uses it for washing dishes, wiping the counters and mopping the floors.

■ Borax is an inexpensive *cleaning agent* that can be purchased in a grocery store. Many people mix borax with water for hard-to-clean areas. Borax is effective when mixed with warm water but borax is a natural mineral and highly toxic so care must be exercised with its use.

■ Use plain old Parson's ammonia with water for just about any *general cleanup* job such as tile, walls and floors in the bathroom and kitchen. If you buy the lemon-scented or pine-scented household ammonia, you are getting great cleanup potential for literally pennies per job and the fresh scent is nice. (*Never* mix ammonia with any other household cleaner.)

■ Kerosene mixed with a bucket of soapy water makes *ring-around-the-bathtub stains* disappear. It is also good for cleaning *cellar steps*.

■ Good old vinegar works for scouring *pots and pans*. Equal parts of salt and vinegar made into a paste will do the trick.

■ Stains are a major reason that clothes have to be discarded long before you intended to replace them. There are many books in the library and articles written in magazines that offer tips for *stain removal*. By treating the stain soon after it occurs you can often save the garment. Post a handy reference in the laundry room that will tell you how to remove chewing gum, grease, grass, blood, crayon and tea stains. One quick example is to rub some cornstarch into a grease or oil mark. Let it set and brush the cornstarch away. Salt can help soak up fresh wine stains. (Check the back of your cookbook for some simple stain removers.)

■ Read *Is There Life After Housework?* by Don Aslett.

■ I used to buy *prewash stain and spot remover*. But I found that if I put a liquid laundry detergent on the stain, let it soak for a few minutes, add a tiny bit of warm water and scrub with a toothbrush, the stain is removed without a trace in most cases.

■ Save leftover pieces of soap to use as a *presoak stain remover* for delicate items or as a soft-scrub mixture to brush against stains. Add boiling water to a jar half-filled with the soap leftovers. When the mixture has a jellylike consistency, use it to pretreat spots before laundering.

■ Rather than trying to wash *mattresses and drapes* with a liquid cleaner or disinfectant, try airing them outside to get rid of the musty smell.

■ I love the convenience of *fabric softener sheets* for the dryer but, for economy, people tell me that using the liquid fabric softener is the better buy. (You must use the amount of liquid suggested to realize the savings. If you use too much, the savings would be marginal.)

■ Make your own cleaner for *wool garments* you wish to launder by hand by mixing 2 tablespoons of a mild dishwashing liquid (not the automatic dishwasher variety) with 3 gallons of lukewarm water. Soak the item inside out for five minutes. Do not wring the garment, but work the suds through. Rinse, and remove excess water by pressing against the side of the sink. Do not hang, but lay the garment flat on towels that will absorb the excess water.

■ Make your own *wood polish* using only white vinegar and safflower oil. You will need two-thirds cup white vinegar and one-third cup safflower oil. Get the blender out and slowly add the safflower oil to the vinegar in the blender. Use as you would any commercial polish for a nice shine. Or try a mixture of ½ quart mineral oil with ½ tablespoon lemon oil, which are both purchased at a drugstore. Spray and wipe with a clean cloth.

■ Saturate a cloth with olive oil to *clean wood furniture* just as if you were using wax polish. Wipe the excess with a clean cloth.

■ Give *leather furniture* a shine by wiping with cotton dipped in vinegar.

■ Acetone *removes contact cement* and wood glue. It can be purchased inexpensively at a hardware store.

■ Not that you would have any ants near your spotless home. . . but did you know you can solve an *ant infestation* problem without sprays or ant traps? Wash the area where the pesky critters are meeting with full-strength white vinegar.

Keep them from entering your home by washing the floors of the entry ways with a few strong coats of white vinegar. The ants will not be eager to pass across that doorway to enter your home because the smell repels them.

This idea seems chancy but it was recommended. Put cucumber peelings mixed with salt wherever the ants congregate, and you won't see them anymore. (What if it were just my luck that the ants in my neighborhood liked cucumbers?)

■ Make sweet-smelling *potpourri* by simmering on the stove 4 teaspoons cinnamon in 4 cups water. Or mix this potpourri for a fresh scent: ¼ cup pine needles, 1 tablespoon whole cloves, ½ cup lemon rind, 3 cinnamon sticks, 2 teaspoons allspice. Mix and save in a pretty tin. When you want a nice fragrance, add three teaspoons of the mixture with 2 cups of cold water. Simmer in a pot on the burner of your stove. Great for a holiday scent and, also, for replacing the leftover odor of a burnt dinner!

■ Mix a small amount of a plain chlorine bleach such as Clorox with warm water and use for *basic household cleaning and disinfecting* (about one part bleach to nine parts water). I use this to wipe spills, the kitchen and bathroom sinks, counters and floors and other washable surfaces.

■ Plain old household salt is an inexpensive *scouring powder*. Just rub as if it were cleanser for cleaning a baking dish.

■ To clean *bathroom sink stains*, mix creme of tartar and hydrogen peroxide (drugstore) to a paste consistency. Use a toothbrush to scrub the stain.

■ And after you've done all this, treat yourself to a scented *bubble bath*. Buy borax at the drugstore, add a drop of food coloring and some perfume. Mix well. Enjoy!

■ *Extra caution*: Never mix household cleaners of any kind.

For families committed to being tight with the buck (by choice or forced by circumstance to adopt the life-style of the Not Rich and Not Famous) these suggestions will save money in a variety of ways. Some people may say that little savings won't even make a dent in their quest to get out of debt. I have been pleasantly surprised on many occasions at how cutting back in little ways can make a big difference in the overall budget. Parents on a budget should probably pay homage to the geniuses who offered the sage advice, "A penny saved is a penny earned!" and "Waste not, want not!" and "Little things make a difference."

To the readers of this book, I would very much like to hear your innovative ways to save and make money. Send your ways to cut costs, obtain free products, save on purchases (large and small) and other cost-saving opportunities you have discovered. I will include them in future editions of this book.

Patricia C. Gallagher
301 Holly Hill Road
Richboro, PA 18954
215-364-2089

Patricia C. Gallagher welcomes interviews and speaking engagements.

email: yngsparro@aol.com
Visit our web site: www.teamofangelshelpme.com